TRANSFORM YOUR PROJECT LEADERSHIP

For Professionals Leading Projects or Company Initiatives

TRANSFORM YOUR PROJECT LEADERSHIP

For Professionals Leading Projects or Company Initiatives

Author and Executive Editor
Naomi R. Caietti, PMP, CTM

1. Business & Economics: Project Management 2. Business & Economics: Leadership 3. Business & Economics: Careers

ISBNS:
Print Edition: 978-0-9600565-0-7
ebook Edition: 978-0-9600565-1-4

Cover design by Lewis Agrell
Edited by Gabriella Caietti

Printed in the United States of America

Treelake Publishing

ACKNOWLEDGEMENT

Leadership is about growing other leaders. Focusing on my own personal growth and helping others achieve success as leaders has been my motivation to write this book. Without the support of all my friends, family and global community of leaders this book would not exist, so I share my gratitude for their enduring inspiration.

To every leader I followed to learn how to lead, every manager who gave me an opportunity to deliver a new product, service or program, and every high performing team I was privileged to learn from; these experiences led me to realize how important leadership and learning were to any individual tasked to lead a project.

To my sponsors who talked about me to advance my career and support me and the team to produce long lasting results, outcomes and value for the organization.

To every project manager (PM) in my global community that partnered to engage in person and online to share my knowledge, influence the practice of project management and careers, one project manager at a time.

To my coaches that helped me push past barriers and obstacles, guided me towards living my vision and values daily to realize my dreams to be a global thought leader.

To my editors, publishers, and organizations for allowing me to promote excellence in project management, leadership and management through global online resources as an author, speaker and digital entrepreneur.

To each of the contributing expert authors of this book who stepped forward to put a pen to paper to share their insights on a timeless leadership tenet.

To John Estrella who graciously authored the foreword for this publication and has served as an inspiration for me personally and professionally for all his great work.

To my publisher/adviser, Stephanie Chandler and her team for their expertise, coaching and industry expertise to elevate and bring my book to my online followers around the globe.

To my family, Chris and Gabby for their daily encouragement, and steadfast support to allow me to live my dreams and help me find the balance in my life's adventures! Also, to my best furry office mates Biskit and Brownie who keep me grounded through their daily inspiration to "wag more and bark less."

"Writing is the painting of the voice." —Voltaire

—Naomi R. Caietti

FOREWORD

Written by an international team of leaders, this book covers the key competencies that one must possess in order to be an effective leader in today's team environments. It starts by highlighting the importance of coaches, mentors and sponsors. Although natural leaders can reach a certain level of success on their own, they need a healthy dose of periodic self-reflections and external guidance in order to take their success to the next level. With third-party support, it will be easier to bridge the gaps in both technical skills and behavioral competencies.

Given that most leaders possess a higher intelligence quotient (IQ), they need to fully comprehend and apply emotional intelligence (EI) to differentiate themselves from their peers. Others have referred to EI as EQ (emotional quotient) and it will not be unusual to hear that "IQ can help you move up in the organization, but EQ can take you even higher." It is worth noting that a higher IQ may not necessarily equate to a higher EQ so be aware of that fact as you progress through the ranks.

There is a saying that states, "You have two ears and one mouth. Use them in proportion." It is refreshing to see an entire chapter devoted to pointing out the importance of listening as a key competency of an effective leader. Active listening skills will allow the leader to influence, motivate, negotiate and resolve conflicts. On top of these skills, a good leader must also be creative in solving problems.

With these key competences covered in detail in this book, you'll be better equipped to lead and manage your team effectively and efficiently. Good luck on your leadership journey!

John A. Estrella, PhD, CMC, PMP
President, Agilitek Corporation

TABLE OF CONTENTS

INTRODUCTION
WELCOME TO THE TRANSFORM YOUR PROJECT LEADERSHIP BOOK!

Have you felt stuck in your personal or professional life looking for guidance on how to move forward? Don't you wish you had a mentor, coach, sponsor or a group of advisors? As a leader are you ready to learn the secrets to *get unstuck*, jumpstart your career and take the first step up towards your journey to *transforming your project leadership*? If you are a professional in your organization tasked to lead projects, manage people, develop processes, launch initiatives, navigate politics and everything in between, this book is for you.

The purpose of this book is to help provide in depth guidance for reflection on leadership, advice to improve skillsets, and close behavioral gaps. It's packed with actionable tips on leadership, advisors, and how to leverage the top ten leadership competencies as identified by the Project Management Institute (PMI) to build a career strategy for new, seasoned and credentialed leaders — *"professionals"* leading projects in their organizations.

Today's leaders should learn to stretch themselves as they move along their career paths. Leaders can't just rely on their tacit know of project management; they must be better leaders who are mindful, open, flexible, empathetic, communicative,

and engaged. Project Management is both an art and science —
a blend of hard and core skillsets.

*"If you just focus on managing a process, you'll be missing
the big picture aspects of project management today —
people." —Naomi R. Caietti, PMP*

What has changed in the last decade that now requires a
leader to have a laser focus on core skills? *Leadership*: direct
and indirect management of people, and *emotional intelligence*: influencing and developing relationships, are the two
top competencies that have become more critical to success
in the management of projects within the last decade.

Several years ago, a study was done by the PMI Leadership
Community of Practice who identified *competency, leadership,* and *emotional intelligence* as the top three indexes that
project/program managers need to excel in to be successful
in their projects. Several years ago, the Project Management
Institute developed a roadmap called the "PMI Talent Triangle"
which can be found at www.pmi.org. This roadmap helps
leaders build a set of skillsets, behaviors, and competencies
that support longer-range strategic objectives, and provides
leaders with the tools to add value as a strategic partner and
help contribute to the organization's bottom line. The PMI
Talent Triangle reflects a combination of technical, strategic,
and business management expertise and is what the ***primary***
focus of this book is about — **leadership**. These are the key
leadership competencies shared in standalone chapters and
throughout this book:

- *Brainstorming, Coaching and Mentoring, Conflict
  Management, Emotional Intelligence, Influencing,
  *Interpersonal Skills, Listening, Negotiating, Problem
  Solving, and Team Building. (*Interpersonal Skills are
  discussed throughout the book)*

Have you asked yourself if you are ready to take the first step up towards your leadership journey, and what is holding you back? Just know that *leadership* is a choice; not a position. You will have many opportunities along your career; it's your choice to pivot and choose the right path. It is the series of choices I made along my career path that helped me to move past obstacles, set lofty goals, get unstuck and inspired me to write this book. I made a commitment to a lofty goal eight years ago when I graduated from PMI Leadership Institute Master Class (LIMC). My goal was to continue to pay it forward, encourage excellence in project management, leadership, and management, and inspired project leaders to lead!

PART 1

Leadership: The Key to Project Success

ARE YOU READY TO LEAD?

Basically, I've learned that leadership is a daily mindful practice and I know that by doing so will help you to transform your project leadership. Project leaders have choices to navigate and can accelerate their career path; this book can be used as a guide to help you *transform your project leadership*. You will move along in your project leadership journey and transform from a tactical to strategic leader. There is nothing more powerful than to reflect back to move forward as you continue down the path on your journey to leadership.

Here are my recommendations for using this book to transform your project leadership and accelerate your growth to be a more competent and strategic leader ready to take on the challenges to lead projects in your organization:

- Read the introduction, and leadership sections (Part 1 and 2). You'll determine how best to approach what you need for just in time, short and long-term goal setting.

- Focus on the ten competencies for project leaders in Chapters 1–10 that will help any leader of projects in any industry. These are proven competencies for any credentialed PMI credential holder, seasoned professional or practitioner.

- Raise your self-awareness through assessment and reflection. You must focus on your individual personal growth and development. There are several assessment tools out there today; review the additional resources and bonus material at the end of the book to take an assessment of your behaviors to receive a detailed analysis.

- Create opportunities to leverage your strengths and minimize your behavioral gaps. As a project leader understand your career path and position yourself to take advantage of these opportunities.

- Identify mentors, coaches or sponsors inside or outside your organization with similar behaviors. Check with your internal organization to determine if they have a mentor program. Many PMI Chapters now have mentor programs to help mentees/protégés. You may have more than one mentor for specific areas of focus i.e.: process, business, politics.

- Work with your mentor/sponsor to select projects and programs to lead that provide opportunities to build targeted skills. You may have to do this internally and externally. Choosing projects that align with your goals may be challenging; it requires support from human resources, management and your project management office. A career path inside your organization is critical to achieve this; however, this can also be achieved by pairing a project manager with a senior project/program manager to shadow a medium or large project with a key role on the team.

- Attend targeted training that will enhance the desired behaviors. You must not wait too long to apply what you have learned; pair the training with a project or initiative. You may have to do this internally or externally.

- Learn more about change, stakeholder engagement models and breakthrough project management.

- Create an action plan to minimize your behavior gaps and facilitate improvement in your delivery of projects/programs in your organization.

- Review the section on "How to Use this Book" including the tips and advice built into each chapter and the additional resources section for bonus material to review and download.

It is the choices we make along the way that will guide us to reach our greatest potential and our lofty goals. We can only realize these choices if we embrace a leadership mindset to reflect to move forward.

It's my hope that this book fills a gap and provides a focus on the key leadership competencies and behaviors project leaders need to develop to be successful today. Be prepared to step up and choose to take every teachable moment as leaders in your organization to shape the maturity of the discipline of project management. Always continue to add value, manage change, measure excellence in your projects through benefit realization, value management and customer satisfaction. Strive to become a more strategic leader by focusing on your leadership daily.

As project leaders every day you should focus on your leadership, partner with your customers to find solutions to their business problems and strive to elevate the discipline of project management to add value. It's just what great leaders do!

WHAT IS TRANSFORMATIONAL LEADERSHIP?

Over the years, I've embraced continuous learning and strive to be a student of life and leadership. I've continued my passion to deliver excellence in project, program, and portfolio management by working with clients like Project Management Institute, Workfront, ProjectManagement.com, and California Virtual Campus Online Education Initiative to name a few. Over the years, I've studied leadership from all aspects and in my own journey into leadership I've adapted many techniques, approaches and styles. I prefer transactional and transformational leadership styles for two reasons. One, these are the two most popular styles for the type of organizations and cultures I've worked in and they served me well in my career as an information technology project manager, consultant and strategic adviser over the years.

Transformational Leadership, a book by authors Bass and Riggio offers this explanation:

> "Transformational leaders are those who stimulate and inspire followers to both achieve extraordinary outcomes and, in the process, develop their own leadership capacity. Transformational leaders help followers grow and develop into leaders by responding to individual follower's needs by empowering them and by aligning the objectives and

goals of the individual followers, the leader, the group, and the larger organization."

In addition, psychologist and leadership expert Ronald E. Riggio reveals in a *Psychology Today* article the following:

"Research evidence clearly shows that groups led by transformational leaders have higher levels of performance and satisfaction than groups led by other types of leaders."

Today's global economic landscape is continuing to change for organizations and project leaders. Organizations need to evolve, change and *transform* to stay relevant in this new global economy, and so do YOU. Transformational leadership is relevant today, tomorrow and in the future. As a project leader you will need to reflect on how you want to transform your project leadership.

"**Leadership and learning** are indispensable to
each other." —John F. Kennedy.

WHY LEADERSHIP SHOULD MATTER TO PROJECT LEADERS

As a thought leader, I'm focused on staying in touch with current trends on leadership from leading experts in the field, conferences, and social media. Earlier this year, I developed and delivered a webinar for Information Technology Metrics and Productivity Institute (ITMPI) to share some insights and perspectives on my new book. Usually during my research for my webinar I find some interesting perspectives that I share with my audiences. These are just a few perspectives to keep in mind that follow as you consider why leadership should matter to you.

Perspective is a leading indicator. One of my favorite quotes I like is "The only place success comes before work is in the dictionary." Recently I read an article by author Bill Treasure that stated, "Leadership that's hard is leadership that's unattractive." This is the perspective of new members of the workforce. His article stated one global study of 2,422 millennials showed that less than 20% of them desire to be a leader at a large organization.

Why? Because they view the traditional role of a leader as one that places too much emphasis on profits and production, and not enough on developing people or contributing to societal good.

Let's look at the landscape — five generations in the workforce, downsized organizations, collapsed roles (jack of all trades/master of none), digital/remote workforce, and limping through another leadership crisis.

Project Managers in any role are facing new and demanding challenges leading projects in organizations in our new global economy. As a project leader your success is defined by time and hard work; it takes time to develop hard and core skillsets, but can you accelerate the learning? The answer is...100% YES!

Five generations; so much to learn from each other, what better time to put in the hard work and lead....

Let me just say that the challenge/struggle/hard work associated with leading others is real and the payoff is in the satisfaction of making a positive difference for the people and the organization you serve.

If you are a professional in your organization tasked to lead projects, manage people, develop processes, initiatives, navigate politics and everything in between, this book is for YOU!

REFLECT TO TRANSFORM YOUR LEADERSHIP

S elf-reflection will be one of the most powerful ways for you to start your transformation. Self-reflection is about asking yourself thoughtful questions that are designed to give insights into how you work: what you do well, and what needs improving.

Many times, kicking off the new year is a great time to reflect on prior experience to move forward and plan some BIG lofty goals. You need to learn to stretch yourself as you move along your career path. Starting after the new year, let's look at how you can kick start your career goals to plan incremental improvements over time.

REFLECT

Take stock of your accomplishments and failures; there is so much to learn by taking this first step early in the year. Besides, it's time to dust off those old habits, wipe the slate clean and start fresh with new goals and objectives.

Here are some questions to reflect on:

- Are you reviewing what you learned through success and failure? Write down your strengths, weaknesses and blind spots and prioritize your goals to improve your skillsets and behaviors.

- Did you experience growth as well as setbacks as a PM professional? Did you achieve all your goals or were they not lofty enough to experience the growth you expected?

- Did you fail to engage with your teams, add value to your customers' strategic objectives and/or earn trust with your stakeholders?

Just know that you need to continue to make improvements to grow into better project leaders.

PLAN SLOW TO MOVE FAST

You should carefully build a strategy for your career and plan for how you are going to reach your goals. Your career is an investment; treat it that way. Here are some planning questions to consider.

- What are your career goals for 2019? i.e.: new job, promotion, reenter the workforce or shift and pivot to a new role in a different industry?

- What do you enjoy doing? Consider your strengths and roles you would do well in.

- What are your weaknesses? Consider training and development necessary to move into roles you are interested in.

- Do you have a mentor, coach or sponsor? A combination of one or more advisors can help you plan a strategic career path.

Personal growth and development are your responsibility; create a group of advisors to help you realize your leadership potential and achieve your career goals faster.

ACT NOW; TIME TO TAKE ACTION

Are you ready? There is no time like the present; obstacles will always be in your way and excuses are just another reason to stifle your personal growth. Get out of your comfort zone and act! Here are some ideas to get you in the positive mindset to take that next step to reach your goals.

- What were some of your obstacles last year that prevented you from achieving your goals? What if you flipped these obstacles into opportunities?

- Do you think you have a growth mindset and can step outside your comfort zone?

- Do you want to try to achieve some big audacious goals this year?

You may need to focus on how to achieve a growth mindset to move past your obstacles and turn them into opportunities.

If you are not doing what you love and love what you are doing daily; isn't it time for a change? Start off the new year by kickstarting your new career goals. You can use these tips as a process to 1) reflect, 2) plan and 3) act to develop an action plan to reach your career goals.

NOTES:

_____

_____

_____

_____

_____

PART 2

A Team of Advisors Can Guide Your Way

1

TRANSFORM YOUR PROJECT LEADERSHIP

Naomi R. Caietti

A s a leader today, do you find it difficult to find influential role models in your organization that can help guide you up the corporate ladder? Are you finding it hard to juggle your job, career and personal life? Don't you wish you knew how to navigate the many obstacles leaders face in their personal and professional lives? Do you wake up wondering why you are not living your perfect life? What is the secret other leaders have discovered to thrive in their current jobs, jumpstart their careers down the right path, and awaken their personal hopes and dreams? Our economy is rebounding with entrepreneurs at the forefront as dynamic drivers of global economic growth. These successful leaders have discovered the secret to greater empowerment, career success, and social capital by building these powerful career relationships. Are you ready to **transform your project leadership**, and **get unstuck** to propel your leadership forward? Today, you can elevate yourself with one or more of these three career development relationships: *coach, mentor* and/or *sponsor.*

> "If you want to be great and successful, choose people who are great and successful and walk side by side with them." —Ralph Waldo Emerson

FIVE STEPS TO PICKING THE RIGHT MENTOR, COACH AND/OR SPONSOR

Finding mentors, coaches and sponsors can be an overwhelming task but research shows that they can make a real difference in our lives. Daniel Coyle, a New York Times bestselling author, shared this tip on how to pick a career development expert:

> *"TIP #12: Five ways to pick a high-quality mentor, coach and/or sponsor*
>
> *1. Avoid Someone Who Reminds You of a Courteous Waiter*
>
> *2. Seek Someone Who Scares You a Little. Look for someone who: Watches you closely, is action-oriented, and is honest, sometimes unnervingly so.*
>
> *3. Seek Someone Who Gives Short, Clear Directions*
>
> *4. Seek Someone Who Loves Teaching Fundamentals*
>
> *5. Other Things Being Equal, Pick the Older Person"*

COACHES, MENTORS AND SPONSORS

The three types of career development relationships as shown in the model below are: Coach, Mentor, and Sponsor.

Career Relationship Model

COACHES, MENTORS, AND SPONSORS
Understanding the Differences

A coach talks to you, a mentor talks with you, and a sponsor talks about you.

* Roles may sometimes overlap

COACH	A coach provides guidance for your development, often focused on soft skills (e.g., active listening) rather than technical skills (e.g., financial acumen).
Who drives the relationship?	You and your coach are responsible for driving the relationship—you can reach out to your coach when you need help, but your coach can also reach out to you.
Actions	Provide development feedback outside the formal performance evaluation process.

MENTOR	A mentor informally or formally helps you navigate your career, providing guidance for career choices and decisions.
Who drives the relationship?	You drive the relationship. Your mentor is reactive and responsive to your needs.
Actions	Help you determine possible career paths to meet specific career goals.

SPONSOR	A sponsor is a senior leader or other person who uses strong influence to help you obtain high-visibility assignments, promotions, or jobs.
Who drives the relationship?	The sponsor drives the relationship, advocating for you in many settings, including behind closed doors.
Actions	Advocate for your advancement and champion your work and potential with other senior leaders.

CATALYST
Changing workplaces Changing lives

Created: 31 December 2014
catalyst.org

Source: Catalyst

You will have many choices in picking the right career development expert to get you to where you want to go. As a mentee or protégé, you should relate to the following tips in this way:

- Get comfortable being out of your comfort zone. Mentors and coaches should push you towards growth and improvement; growth and comfort don't exist together. (Tip #1)

- Look for coaches and sponsors who want to understand your motivations, commitment, and are laser focused on action and giving immediate and honest feedback. (Tip #2)

- Great mentors, coaches and sponsors give brief, short, and clear useful information. (Tip #3)

- Get good at fundamental skillsets and behaviors, practice with your mentor and coach so you can step up to greater challenges and leverage your talent. (Tip #4)

- Great mentors, coaches and sponsors are first and foremost lifelong learners with broad based experience and a variety of perspectives. (Tip #5)

A CASE FOR SPONSORSHIP?

Lately, there has been much conversation around the importance of having a mentor, coach and/or sponsor versus a mentor to advance your career.

Recent research done on the impact of sponsorship for career advancement shares these insights:

- Men and women with sponsors are 23% more like to advance in their careers than those without sponsors. —Center for Talent Innovation

- Career sponsorship can increase the ability to land a raise or stretch assignment by 30% —Hewlett

- Men are 46% more likely than women to have a career sponsor. —Hewlett

- Women are more likely to have mentors than male counterparts, but mentorship does not have the same impact as sponsorship. —Catalyst

FIVE TIPS ON HOW FIND AND ATTAIN A CAREER SPONSOR?

Perhaps the most groundbreaking research about sponsorship has been written about in Sylvia Anne Hewlett's new book, "Forget a Mentor; Find a Sponsor." Hewlett shares many lessons for men and women to leverage their careers to new heights by focusing on a sponsor instead of a mentor. The great news is that you can choose one or more career development relationships along your unique journey.

Hewlett's recent research strongly urges for men and women to follow these five steps to find and develop a relationship with a sponsor to profoundly shift your career:

1. *Join Networks Filled with Influential People.* Finding a sponsor within a corporate structure or join a not-for-profit board in your field where you'll likely meet others in your industry, Hewlett suggests.

2. *Build Trust First.* Sponsors are putting their own reputation on the line when they suggest you for a promotion, job, or opportunity. "Trust is as important as performance," says Hewlett.

3. *Turn Mentors into Sponsors.* Identifying someone who could be a great sponsor, and first asking that person to mentor you, Hewlett suggests.

4. ***Sponsors are Gatekeepers.*** Sponsors are in a position of power to help you advance your career. "You do not need to like your sponsor," says Hewlett. Sponsors can be gatekeepers to your next promotion, round of funding, or significant career move.

5. ***Remember It's an Agreement.*** Research has shown that leaders who sponsor do better themselves than those who don't sponsor. "The big principle is to give before you get," says Hewlett.

"Sponsors, not mentors, put you on the path to power and influence by three things: pay raises, high-profile assignments, and promotions." —Sylvia Ann Hewlett

TRANSFORM YOUR PROJECT LEADERSHIP

As a leader recognize that leadership is a choice not a position. It's your choice to choose to step up to lead, move past obstacles to light your torch, *transform your project leadership,* and find great coaches, mentors and/or sponsors to guide you in your career journey. As a leader, recognize what made you successful today, may not make you successful in the future. Focus on your vision to build your successful life which includes your job, career and the balance you seek in life. Foster these new relationships with your mentors, coaches and sponsors; a new personal board of advisors that will act as a collaborative of wisdom, knowledge and experience for you to tap into to reach your vision. Improvement is the focus of learning and improving yourself is the first step to improving everything else.

Be honest with yourself & transformation is possible.
—Anonymous

CREATE YOUR PERSONAL VISION

First things first, focus on your personal vision since this will be your guide for a mentor, coach and especially your sponsor to help you leverage your career success. Your personal vision defines your dreams to build *your successful career* and if you want to accelerate your career faster; pick a sponsor. We all have dreams and passions about career, life and work. Today, leaders are learning new skills and behaviors on the job, looking for opportunities to advance up the career ladder and trying to maintain a work-life balance.

The real key to turn your dreams into reality is to develop a personal vision statement. A persuasive vision can help you succeed personally and professionally and get the most out of your career relationships with a mentor, coach and/or sponsor. A personal vision statement is a paragraph that encapsulates everything you would like to be, do, and have in your career. It defines what success and excellence looks like to you. It expresses your vision for where you want to be in the future and it reflects your values, goals, and purpose for your life.

DEVELOP YOUR PERSONAL VISION STATEMENT

Answer these six questions to explore ideas for your statement:

1. What are the eight things you enjoy doing?

2. What three things must you do every single day to feel fulfilled in your life and work?

3. What are your five-six *most important values*?

4. If you never had to work another day in your life; what would you do choose to do that you enjoy doing?

5. What strengths do others see in you? What strengths do you see in yourself?

6. What goals do you want to achieve in the next 6 months, 3 years or 5 years?

NOTES:

_____

_____

WRITE YOUR PERSONAL VISION STATEMENT

Now that you've learned more about yourself, you can write your own vision statement. Let's review the following things you've discovered about yourself:

My inspirations that motivate/bring me happiness and fulfillment:

My greatest strengths/abilities/traits/things I do best:

Two or more strengths to use more often and bring me happiness:

My Personal Vision Statement for myself (in 50 words or less):

_____

_____

_____

_____

Examples of a personal vision statement:

"To inspire project leaders around the globe to step up and lead." —*Naomi Caietti*

"To serve as a leader, live a balanced life, and apply ethical principles to make a significant difference." —*Denise Morrison*

"To use my gifts of intelligence, charisma, and serial optimism to cultivate the self-worth and net-worth of women around the world." —*Amanda Steinberg*

Personal Empowerment Action Plan Worksheet:
Personal empowerment begins with integrating these new relationships with your mentor, coach and/sponsor into your day to day life. Your personal growth and development should be a daily focus and it's important to have a template to manage your progress.

Consider all the aspects of your life that you want to improve, shift or pivot to learn how to manage life's obstacles, new skillsets/behaviors and step up to new leadership roles in your organization.

Below is a template example.

Type	Commitment	Start Date	Resources
Work-Life	*How to incorporate healthy exercise into my schedule?*	May	Mentor – Pam
	As a parent, how do I manage my career and family demands of my childcare?	June	Mentor - Sue
Job	*How do I motivate my project team?*	Ongoing	Coach - Bob
	What do I need to learn about new IT processes?	Ongoing	Mentor - Kyle
	How do I get my projects done on schedule, on budget and meets customer needs?	Ongoing	Coach - Kim
Career	*How do I get my next promotion? What are my skill gaps?*	Jan.	Coach/ Sponsor - Ann
	How can I improve my organizational awareness and build relationships with senior leaders? How can I be aware of my blind spots?	Jan.	Mentor/ Sponsor - Dan

NOTES:

_____

_____

_____

Resources and Recommended Reading:

"Bridging the PM Competency Gap" by Loredana Abramo and Richard Maltzman

"Developing Successful Career Relationships: Leveraging Mentoring, Coaching, and Sponsorship" by Sarah Kalicin

"Finding Your Voice" edited by Linda Eastman

"Forget a Mentor; Find a Sponsor" by Sylvia Ann Hewlett

"The Little Book of Talent: 52 Tips for Improving Your Skills" by Daniel Coyle

"Transformational Leadership" by Bernard Bass and Ronald Riggio

ABOUT THE AUTHOR
NAOMI R. CAIETTI, PMP CTM

Naomi Caietti is a widely-respected thought leader in project management. As the Founder and Director of Naomi Caietti Consulting, Naomi offers virtual services to niche clients. She is a sought-after speaker, coach and published author, and has spoken to thousands of project managers around the globe. Since leaving her corporate position to start her own business in 2014, Naomi has worked with a diverse range of clients including corporate, entrepreneurial and private individuals. She was the founder of a women's networking group called "The Glass Breakers," a global group of ten powerful women business leaders in the areas of projects, leadership and management.

Before she started her own company, Naomi had more than 25 years' corporate experience as a credentialed project manager in a public, private, and nonprofit sector focused on managing high visibility enterprise information technology (IT) implementations in key industries. She has been recognized for her work with clients in the public sector, being a key expert on talent, change and career development for ProjectManagement.com, and influential project manager on Twitter (PMOT). Naomi is a graduate from California State University, Sacramento. She is a credentialed project management professional (PMP), graduate of the Project Management Institutes' Leader Institute Master Class (LIMC) and a competent Toastmaster (CTM). Naomi is a 2018 honoree in the book *Woman Kind* by Ferguson and Fox, 2016 recipient of Women of Influence award from ProjectManagers. org and 2013 recipient of a Women in Project Management and #PMChat Influencer award from PDUotd.org. Naomi has co-authored numerous books, among which are *Finding Your Voice, The Assertive and Empowered Woman, The Project Manager Who Smiled, Lessons Learned in Project Management, Bridging the PM Competency Gap, Waterfall to Agile: Lessons from 20 Experts*, and *Project Leadership: Lessons from 40 PPM Experts*.

Naomi's passionately committed to make project leaders successful, inspire women to lead and be a voice for project leaders around the globe.

Contact:

Naomi Caietti Consulting

Email: NaomiCaietti@gmail.com |
   Website: www.naomicaietti.com

Social Media: Linked In: linkedin.com/in/naomicaietti |
   Twitter: www.twitter.com/naomi_caietti

PART 3

CORE LEADERSHIP COMPETENCIES AND BEHAVIORS TO INCREASE YOUR COMPETITIVE EDGE

2

KEEP CALM AND BRAINSTORM

Deanne Earle

Meet regularly with your business team and brainstorm. Intricate business problems are mostly resolved at brainstorming sessions —Richard Branson

Many would have us think there's nothing new and therefore little to learn on the topic of brainstorming, but particularly as people, on their own or in groups, have been using the technique since time began. Yet leaders who think brainstorming is simply an idea generation technique, are ignoring its wider value. Brainstorming is not only a way to generate ideas, it also provides leaders the opportunity to:

- level the creativity field; no one person is too important or insignificant to contribute

- empower participants through listening; people feel like they're part of the process ~ *Refer to Chapter Leaders Listen by Todd Williams*

- turn employees into imagination machines

To get the most out of brainstorming it's not only important to understand how it works, but equally important to appreciate the context of its origins.

The term '***brainstorm***' was first coined by Alex Faickney Osborn (1888-1966) in *Your Creative Power* (originally published in 1940). Osborn, an Advertising Executive frustrated by both the quantity and quality of ideas being generated by people on their own, experimented with different methods during creative problem-solving group sessions. In his book, he describes these group sessions as "the participants should engage in a "brainstorm" — using the brain to storm a creative problem — and doing so in commando fashion, with each stormer attacking the same objective" (chapter 33).

While the act of brainstorming may have been labelled by Osborn in the 1940's, the word brainstorm originated in 1890-95 with a very different meaning. Today's sensitivities and focus on diversity has many organisations and leaders avoiding the word in an attempt not to offend. Whether called *thought shower*, *blue sky thinking*, or *brainstorming*, the process, as developed and used 80+ years ago by Alex Osborn, remains recognisable today.

The standard model of brainstorm — gathering a group of people together and maximising the time available to generate as many ideas as possible in an atmosphere free of criticism or judgement — is not always appropriate or effective for the topic. being stormed. Before scheduling time and gathering participants together, leaders need to think about **WHY** a brainstorm session is needed and **HOW** they're going to create the best possible conditions for it to be successful. Only once these two aspects have been considered can leaders identify and use the appropriate format. An organised group session may be the default but brainstorming is equally effective through:

- chance encounters;
- individuals storming on their own; or
- a goal so specific it serves as a singular reference point for thought and action.

As well as defining the why, how and structure, leaders should think about the wider benefits and various flaws of brainstorming.

RECOGNISING THE WIDER BENEFITS

If the aim of brainstorming is to generate ideas, the purpose is to let creativity shine. Shifting leadership to focus on this purpose enables several often-overlooked benefits to rise to the surface, including:

- Levelling the playing field — it's an opportunity to remove barriers and create equality amongst participants
- Participants get to meet peers they may otherwise not encounter — it's a forum through which people can develop new working relationships and learn about others ability and knowledge
- Contagion and chain reaction — participants feed off each other's ideas, extrapolating existing or generating new ones
- Developing a participant's ability to think - Obvious answers aren't the only answers,

- e.g.: blue = sky but blue can equally = jazz or cheese

- The volume of ideas generated may create opportunities or resolve other challenges

- Freeing up thinking and creativity beyond the brainstorm session

- Building energy and anticipation during it helps sustain engagement and momentum afterwards

- Providing an opportunity to train and mentor future leaders; not only in brainstorming techniques but in the psychology of human interaction and team dynamics

Make It Yours: Take some time to reflect on these benefits as you think about:

- What value they could bring to your leadership

- How recognising them could change your approach to brainstorming

- What would be possible if these benefits were actively targeted

Write your thoughts in a notebook or on a pad. Beside these thoughts list specific actions you could take next time you're organising or participating in a brainstorm.

DON'T IGNORE THE FLAWS

For all the benefits of brainstorming, there is evidence that it doesn't work well. Leadership plays a role in this failure because of the way brainstorming is implemented and conducted or when there's a fixation on one specific method at the expense of others. Ask any employee about their experience of brainstorming and they'll likely confirm that pushing people in to a session is counterproductive. Yes, some ideas will come but most participants bring their normal work context with them therefore contributions are within their frame of reference, role, knowledge, behaviour, and the organisations cultural norms.

Other common flaws associated with brainstorming are:

- Poorly stated problem statements or questions

- Poor facilitation; those in leadership or senior positions are not always the best choice

- The approach being used isn't appropriate for the participants, situation or problem statement; scientific research confirms that the brain doesn't make connections in a rigid / pre-defined atmosphere

- Risk of group-think — harmony and coherence are valued over accurate analysis and critical evaluation. Individuals unquestioningly follow the word of the leader or dominant participant.

- Idea collision — participants awaiting their turn lose their train of thought

- Early ideas have a disproportionate influence over others

- Real or perceived peer pressure to conform

- One or a few people talking and dominating the session leaves others wondering why they're there. Research indicates that in a typical 6-person group / meeting:

- Potential for mundane associations and a focus on low-hanging fruit

- Participants succumbing to the Pollyanna syndrome, i.e.: not wanting to hurt others' feelings

- There is no clear separation between the idea generation activity of brainstorming and the sorting, assessing, selecting ideas process.

Make It Yours: Take some time to reflect on these flaws as you think about:

What impact they could have on your leadership

How recognising them could change your approach to brainstorming

What would be possible if these flaws were actively targeted

Write your thoughts in a notebook or on a pad. Beside these thoughts list specific actions you could take next time you're organising or participating in a brainstorm.

LOOK BEYOND THE OBVIOUS

Creativity is not the domain of one single person. *Through free-association of thoughts and brainstorming, an accidental suggestion can be the best solution* —Joshua Fernandez

The 4 basic rules of brainstorming are well documented and easy to remember:

- focus on quantity not quality

- no criticism or judgement

- encourage 'wild' ideas

- combine and improve, expand, extrapolate on ideas

These rules are universal and apply in all brainstorming situations. Take Pixar as an example. Steve Jobs believed the best meetings happen by accident and when they do, unexpected conversations take place, creativity shines and ideation happens. He purposely created the conditions for this at Pixar by positioning all meeting rooms, eating areas, and even the bathrooms, in a central atrium. This forced people to go to or pass through the atrium for almost everything and, as a result, they'd run into other people, talk and, well, ideate. Jobs created the conditions for Pixar employees to brainstorm ideas in a free-wheeling kind of way any time of the day whenever they met.

Then there's Emirates Team New Zealand cycling their way to America's Cup victory in 2017. When Sir Peter Blake first got involved just before the 1992 challenge, he set one goal that to this day remains the reference point for every idea, decision or investment made by Team New Zealand — "Will it make the boat go faster?" With this goal firmly entrenched, his leadership created the conditions for wild ideas to be brainstormed and pursued; ideas that when taken to the extreme have been radically innovative. Though many teams competing in the 2017 challenge considered a cycling setup over that of the traditional grinder, Team New Zealand were the only ones to turn this seemingly wild idea into a solution that delivered outstanding success; it made the boat go faster.

Not every leader has the luxury of a site build to create the type of conditions Jobs did at Pixar. Nor is it always possible to define such a specific goal as Sir Peter Blake did. Even so, there are alternatives to the status quo model.

BRAINSTORMING UNPLUGGED: TIPS AND TECHNIQUES

Leigh Thompson, J.J Gerber Professor at Kellogg Northwestern University, advocates **brainwriting** (the simultaneous *written* generation of ideas) over **brainstorming** (the simultaneous *oral* generation of ideas). Brainwriting is when leaders or facilitators have participants focus first on writing without interruption. Because no one in the room is talking there's nothing to block the flow of ideas. The important leadership factor in brainwriting is to leave participants writing for a fixed time at the beginning of the session. Only when that time's up are ideas put up on the wall. Typically, a leader will allocate too much time to brainstorming. 10 minutes is a good starting allocation because when participants have too much time they quickly run out of steam and Thompson's research has shown that 75% of ideas generated come out in the first 50% of the meeting time.

% of Ideas Generated 1 Hour Brainstorm

25%

75%

- First 30 mins (or less)
- Last 30 mins (or more)

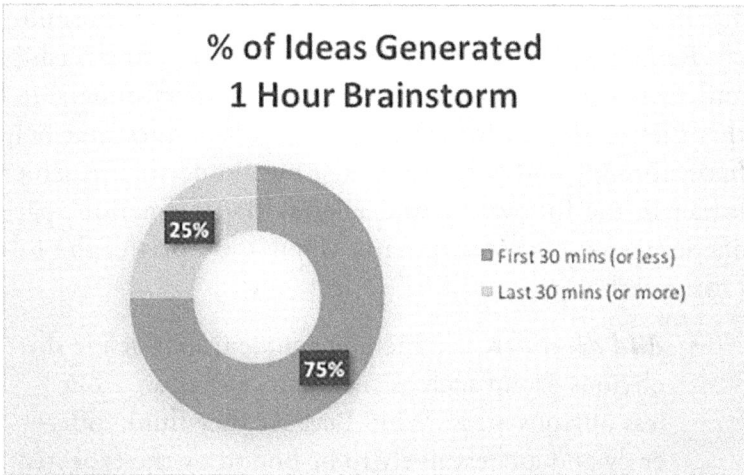

Take Away: Think and plan brainstorming sessions carefully, particularly the amount of time being allotted. More time doesn't lead to more ideas.

One study looked at the first rule of brainstorming: focus on quantity not quality. The results showed that when a quantity goal was a focus for groups, they generated more ideas and ideas of a higher quality than those from groups focused on a quality goal. When leaders focus on quantity the other rules naturally follow as participants are unlikely to criticise or judge which allows wild ideas to emerge.

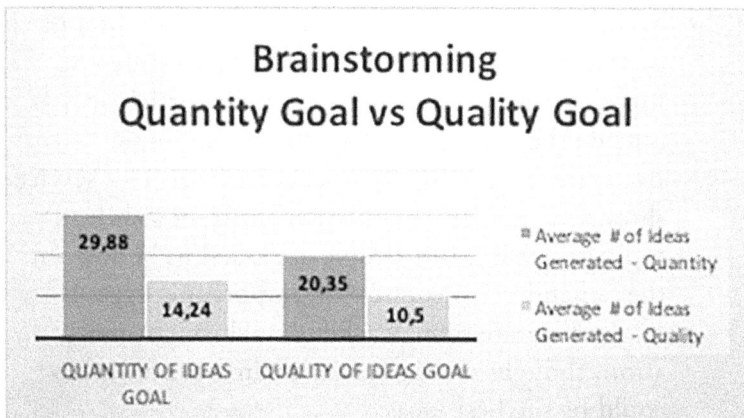

Brainstorming Quantity Goal vs Quality Goal

29,88

20,35

14,24

10,5

- Average # of Ideas Generated - Quantity
- Average # of Ideas Generated - Quality

QUANTITY OF IDEAS GOAL   QUALITY OF IDEAS GOAL

Take Away: Don't ignore the basic rules of brainstorming. Remember there's no one-size-fits-all way of leadership, and so it is with brainstorming. Once leaders understand this they're able to incorporate other techniques that help brainstorming and transforms their own leadership. A senior leader in the Innovation and Digital Transformation space encourages others incorporate, when appropriate, the following techniques:

- *Add diversity*, i.e.: include people from outside the obvious group such as customers and those from less obvious areas. Why? Because they think differently and are less likely to be bound by the expected or status quo options.

- *Take participants through the existing or a possible journey* for the current state where, to start, only questions can be asked. It's a good way to stimulate thinking prior to the actual brainstorm.

- *Look at the actual Customer experience.* Watch a video or request an in-situ demonstration of the customer using the thing / process / service. This gives first-hand insight into the customer experience, helping clarify and define the real problem.

- *Shake things up* to develop agility of thought and approach. Change teams around. Add a different topic or problem into the mix. Push participants outside their standard thinking. For example: Brainstorming better approaches to customer service through a call centre could benefit from a shift in topic mid-way when people are asked to brainstorm the benefits to consumers of, say, organic eggs. It might generate some wacky ideas through association, thought contagion, or chain reactions, they could be the best ideas.

- Go to or hold an *Unconference*. It's a model at
  the bigger end of the brainstorming scale typically
  featuring open discussions rather than the standard
  conference format; exactly what a good brainstorming session should be.

Take Away: Be bold; add other techniques into the brainstorming mix.

Individual brainstorming can be equally as effective as
group brainstorming. Leaders need to support and provide
the space for it. An Entrepreneur and Business Owner in the
Insurance sector uses and encourages others to:

- *Create space for patterns and connections to
  emerge.* Move to a quiet space where with a clear
  head, creativity can shine. With a mixed pile of mag-
  azines, trade journals, hobby or business publications
  at hand, cut words, colours, and images from them
  without judging or editing (those basic brainstorming rules again…); free-wheeling at its finest. With
  a stack of cuttings a few inches thick, spread them
  out looking for patterns and unexpected associations.
  Use a magnetic or pin board to move things around.
  Leave it for a while then come back. See what sur-
  faces for further action.

- *Keep a whiteboard marker in the shower* and write
  notes on the shower glass (do not write on the tiles
  and grout!). A great way to capture thoughts and
  ideas first thing in the morning when the mind is
  open, not stressed by the pressures of the day.

- *Let the board or wall do the work.* Put cuttings
  or post-it notes up in an open area making them
  visible to anyone going past. Casual observers may
  see trends where those close to the topic may not,

or chain reactions could trigger from a 'what would happen if…' comment.

Take Away: Allow time and quiet space for creativity to shine.

Make It Yours: Take some time to reflect on these tips as you think about:

What affect these could have, positive or negative, on your leadership

How they could change your approach to brainstorming

What are you willing to try? Why / Why not?

Write your thoughts in a notebook or on a pad. Beside these thoughts list specific actions you could take next time you're organising or participating in a brainstorm.

TAKE ACTION AND TRANSFORM

The best way to have a good idea is to have lots of ideas
—Linus Pauling

Brainstorming remains a useful tool for generating lots of ideas. Leaders, teams and organisations that benefit the most from it are those willing to challenge the standard model, explore and try different techniques, involve others who are not obvious participants, and, perhaps most importantly of all, create the conditions within which ideas can be freely expressed and explored. Leaders willing to constructively challenge how they approach brainstorming will ask provoking questions, objectively analyse their leadership behaviours, and put together an action plan that will transform not only their leadership but the leadership skills of those around them.

Whether group, individual, or unexpected …

Recommended Reading / Links

Lafley, A G and Charan, R (2008) *The Game-Changer* – How Every Leader Can Drive Everyday Innovation

Osborne, A *The Osborn Checklist: A Creativity Method from the Originator of Brainstorming* [online] http://www. everup.com/2016/01/29/alex-osborn-checklist-traditional-brainstorming/

Paulus, P B, Kohn, N W and Arditti, L E *Effects of Quantity and Quality Instructions on Brainstorming* [online] https:// onlinelibrary.wiley.com/doi/full/10.1002/j.2162-6057. 2011.tb01083.x

Thompson, L – J. Jay Gerber Professor of Dispute Resolutions and Organisations, Northwestern Kellogg University [online]

http://www.kellogg.northwestern.edu/faculty/directory/thompson_leigh.aspx

Video: How brainwriting can neutralise the loudmouths http://www.kellogg. northwestern.edu/news_articles/2014/06 262014-video-thompson-brainwriting.aspx

Unconference.net [online] http://unconference.net/

ABOUT THE AUTHOR
DEANNE EARLE

Deanne Earle is an independent executive level professional with over 20 years of international experience in management, leadership and delivery of large-scale technology-driven change initiatives. The Principal Consultant and Owner of Unlike Before, she is a global expert practitioner who builds the structures and leads the interventions that deliver sustainable change. Deanne is passionate about change-centric thinking and helps companies ensure business readiness in parallel to leveraging the full value of IT.

Effective at both strategic and operational levels, Deanne's broad business skills and knowledge has developed through her work with clients in various roles involving multi-cultural, -lingual, and –national teams around the world and across sectors. She's a published author, speaker, and sought-after contributor across the spectrum of IT PMO's, portfolio, programme and project delivery.

A graduate of Auckland University of Technology in New Zealand, Deanne holds a Diploma in Business along with a Diploma in Management from the New Zealand Institute of Management.

Contact Information:

Deanne Earle
via San Rocco
Rodello (CN) 12050
Italy

+39 3664 537897

Email: dcearle@unlikebefore.com

Website: www.unlikebefore.com | www.deanneearle.eu

Social Media: Twitter: @UnlikeBefore

LinkedIn: https://www.linkedin.com/in/unlikebeforeltd/

Change Through Action Blog http://unlikebefore.
blogspot.com/

3

SELF LEADERSHIP: COACH YOUR WAY TO SUCCESS!

Elise Stevens

Why is coaching an important part of being an exceptional Project Leader?

Coaching forms an essential part of getting the team to work to its full potential. Delivering effective change needs people to work together, with collaboration and working towards a common goal crucial in successfully delivering the project.

for time sensitive project managers, coaching may feel like another task lumped on top of more project-specific activities. Instead, take the view that making the time to grow the skills of individual team members, creating an environment where your people feel valued, inspiring them, and getting the best from your team are all part of your path to becoming a great coach and an exceptional Project Leader.

If you're new to the concept of coaching, it can be hard to

know where to start. Here are my 5 essential tips for incorporating coaching into your project leadership style:

- Tip 1 – Understand Yourself First
- Tip 2 – Your Team is Your Partner
- Tip 3 – Develop a Coaching Plan
- Tip 4 – Implement Your Coaching Plan
- Tip 5 – Include Review and Improve Steps

Scale the coaching activities according to the size of your project. A larger more complex project may require more intensive coaching.

TIP 1 – UNDERSTAND YOURSELF FIRST

Being a good coach involves understanding the needs/opportunities of the people you are coaching and yourself.

One method to understand more about yourself is to undertake a SWOT analysis. SWOT stands for:

- Strengths
- Weaknesses/Challenges
- Opportunities
- Threats

There are many ways to undertake a SWOT analysis on yourself. Some suggested approaches might include:

- Using idea generation techniques
- Reviewing your current and previous performance reviews
- Asking your mentor/manager/team/colleagues

When developing your own SWOT analysis, here are some ideas to consider:

What are my *Strengths* as a Leader/Coach? e.g. • Passion • Communication • Delegation • Creativity • Motivation	What are my *Weaknesses/ Challenges* as a Leader/ Coach? e.g. • Get caught up in the detail • Consistent communication • Learning to trust the team to deliver • Micromanager
What are my *Opportunities for Improvement* as a Leader/Coach? e.g. • Be more consistent • Formalise coaching activities • Push away the negativity • Celebrate successes • Dealing with performance issues in a timely manner	What are my threats as a Leader/Coach? e.g. • Organizational culture • Other change initiatives • Politics

The SWOT analysis will assist you to understand what makes you the leader/coach you are.

Using the output of your SWOT analysis, identify your *Opportunities for Improvement* and *Weaknesses/Challenges* and develop an improvement plan for yourself. Taking time to understand yourself from a technical and soft skills perspective is important. This enables you to understand where you currently are, what your goals are and the approach you are going to use to achieve them.

TIP 2 – YOUR TEAM IS YOUR PARTNER

Remember that when people are not involved in designing and implementing the change, they're less likely to accept it. When people contribute to all aspects of the change, they will own the change and ensure it is a success.

Similarly, from a coaching perspective, it is important to involve the team on the journey as well.

It is important to take into consideration the dynamics of the team. The team environment/function is crucial to developing the approach on how to engage the team in this process.

The following 6 step process provides a framework for establishing a partnership with the individual team members and the team:

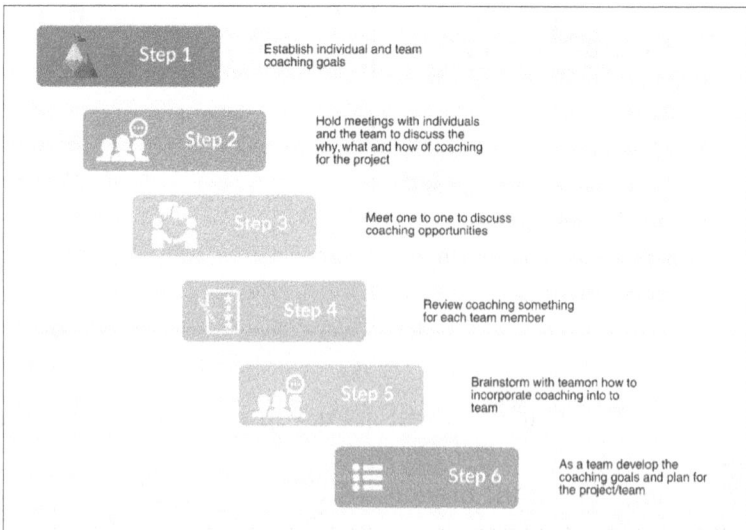

Step 1 — Establish individual and team coaching goals

Step 2 — Hold meetings with individuals and the team to discuss the why, what and how of coaching for the project

Step 3 — Meet one to one to discuss coaching opportunities

Step 4 — Review coaching something for each team member

Step 5 — Brainstorm with team on how to incorporate coaching into to team

Step 6 — As a team develop the coaching goals and plan for the project/team

Step 1 – Establish Individual and Team Goals

People sometimes need something to review and/or critique before they can identify goals. Spending a small amount of time identifying and documenting some goals may assist in moving the process along.

Some example goals are:

- Increase the process knowledge of all team members

- Improve communication skills by 10%

- Knowledge sharing of new technology concepts to be provided by the technology SMEs at key milestone points in the project

Step 2- Hold meetings with Individuals and the Team to discuss the Why, What and How of Coaching for the Project

People will have lots of questions. Often there is a fear of something new and this can often manifest itself into people being negative, dismissive of the initiative and/or change resistant.

Getting the group together to discuss what the challenges the team faces and how we can work together to resolve them through coaching.

This session can be used to ignite the spark of hope in the team about being collaborative. Some concepts to collaborate on include:

- What are the challenges that the team faces to deliver the project?

- Are there any skill gaps?

- What the opportunities for the team?

- What are the short-term goals for the team?

- What are the long-term goals for the team?

- What are the individual challenges for each team member?

- What are the team behaviours that are important?

This information can be shared on the project site so that all team members are engaged with the process.

Step 3 – Meet One on One to Discuss Coaching Opportunities
Meet one to one to discuss what the individual team members are seeking from the project and how coaching can help them achieve their goals. You also need to understand people's current skill levels.

Step 4 – Review Coaching Approach for Each Team Member
Review each team member's goals, aspirations and attitudes to coaching. This will assist in developing the initial draft of the coaching plan.

Step 5 – Brainstorm How to Incorporate Coaching into Team Dynamics
Get the team back together and collectively work out how to achieve the goals that have been established. Initially this should be a stand-alone session. Once completed it should then be included in the regular team meetings and regular one to one meetings.

Step 6 – Develop Coaching Goals and Plan
Formalise the coaching goals and plans for individuals and the team. Include them in project development plans. If you have a matrix / cross functional team speak to the Line Manager about what is going on as well.

TIP 3 – TAKE TIME TO UNDERSTAND YOUR TEAM

In projects we take time to asses our stakeholders, to understand their attitudes and level of support for the project. Undertaking the same analysis for the team involved in delivering the project is just as important. From a team perspective we are assessing the individuals and the team dynamics.

Things to consider include:

- Assess where you think the team is now. This may include

  - Level of cohesiveness

  - Do we have the required skills to deliver the project?

  - What are the growth opportunities for the team?

- Get the team to complete online assessments to understand where they are from a technical and soft skills perspective. Examples are:

  - Gallup International

  - Change Leaders

  - Myers Briggs

- Develop a picture of the team, the project and what challenges/opportunities are now, and in the future

- Be the one to promote open and honest communication

TIP 4 – DEVELOPING A COACHING PLAN IS IMPORTANT TO ENSURING YOUR COACHING GOALS ARE ACHIEVED

Now that the coaching goals have been established collaboratively by the team, and the skills baseline completed, the coaching action plan can be established for the team and for each person.

At this stage, the coaching action plan should only be draft.

Ensure the team related coaching plan is developed in consultation with either the whole team or agreed representatives of the team

- What are the options available for your coaching?

- What are the roles that your team can play in coaching one another?

- What the tactical steps you are going to use to deliver your coaching?

- Develop coaching plans for each team member and stakeholder

TIP 5 – IMPLEMENT YOUR COACHING ACTION PLAN

- Consider your coaching style needs

- Deliver the coaching action plan

- Give the coaching action plan the support and time it needs to grow and take hold

- Encourage the team to do this as well and follow up

Remember to frequently take the time to meet with the team as well as individual team members.

TIP 6 – INCLUDE A REVIEW AND IMPROVE STEP IN YOUR COACHING APPROACH

Once the plan is being delivered, it is important to review the progress against the plan. Is the plan delivering the results you expected? Like Agile retrospective, in this activity it's important to review the past so that we can refine our approach. The information obtained in this process will be used to improve the coaching plan.

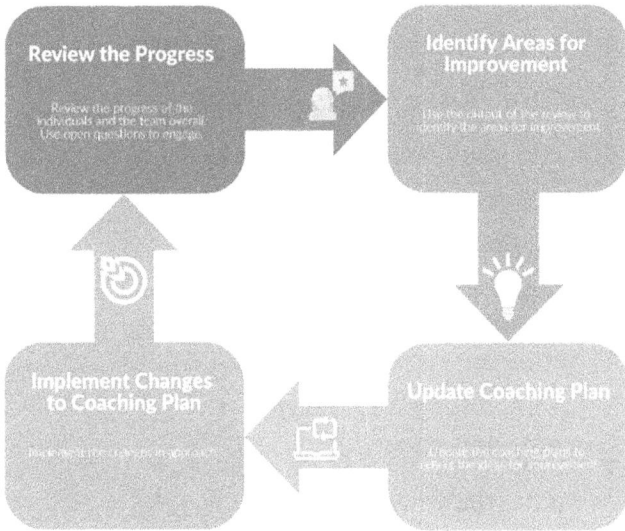

The review sessions should be held progressively throughout the life of the project. The value of these sessions will be reduced if you wait until the end of the end of the project. The opportunity to improve the approach to coaching for the current project will be lost.

It is recommended that reviews be conducted with individual team members and the team.

For larger and/or complex projects, it is suggested that reviews be scheduled at key milestones to gain maximum benefit from the review process.

Step 1 - Review the Progress
Here are 5 open questions for you to assess the progress achieved:

- What were the successes?
- What were the challenges?
- What have you learnt since the last review?
- What would you do differently?
- How do you feel about the project?

Step 2 – Identify Areas for Improvement
Here are 5 open questions for you to use identify areas for improvement:

- What are 3 simple things we can do to improve the coaching approach?
- What are the constraints that are being encountered?
- What are the biggest challenges that are being encountered?
- How can we simplify the coaching approach?
- What is your top improvement idea?

Step 3 – Update Coaching Plan
Update the coaching plan for all members of the team and the overall coaching plan for the team.

TRANSFORM YOUR PROJECT LEADERSHIP

Step 4 - Implement Changes to the Coaching Plan
Start working on the updated activities and approaches in the updated coaching plan.

I believe that delivering successful long-term change requires inspirational leadership from our Project Managers. Incorporating coaching into your leadership style is a key skill that will enable you to become a leader of choice.

NAOMI R. CAIETTI, PMP, CTM

ABOUT THE AUTHOR
ELISE STEVENS

I work with women in project management roles to reinforce within themselves their true value to their team, company and industry. I provide a channel for women's voices to be heard, supported and embraced in project management. It's time for women to dream big in the industry, and to know that they can achieve their career goals.

While women have been recognised as equals throughout various industries in recent years, the number of women in the project management field has barely risen. There is a reason for this.

I work with incredible women who have extensive knowledge, skills and passion for their career, but unfortunately the high pressure and status quo within the workplace has left them feeling emotionally exhausted; they have lost confidence in their own hard-earned skills and are considering leaving their roles.

For over two decades, I have worked closely with project managers to positively impact and innovate effective management processes. I have collaborated with a range of organizations including Queensland Urban Utilities, Ipswich City Council, Coca-Cola Amatil, Hutchinson Telecoms and Ansett Australia.

Contact:

Name: Elise Stevens

Email: elise@elisestevens.co |
    Website: www.elisestevens.co

Phone: 61 433 375 824

Social Media: | Twitter: @elisethepm
    LinkedIn: https://www. linkedin.com/in/elisestevens/

4

MOVING FROM CONFLICT TO COLLABORATION

Ray Frohnhoefer

As a leader, you have a responsibility to bring together teams and other groups of people to accomplish a common goal. Sounds easy right? But teams go through developmental stages and groups form and disband all the time, often without achieving their purpose. What stands in the way of your success? One word: CONFLICT. Conflict turns our workplaces and organizations into battlefields.

Conflict is one of mankind's original issues. Just look at the sacred books of any of the world's religions. There are conflicts between the original man and woman and their god(s), and it only gets more intense from there. Conflict can occur in many "degrees" ranging from simple disagreements to all-out war. Today conflict exists in every team and organization. And, depending on your religious viewpoints on the passage of time from creation, it has had thousands, if not tens and hundreds of thousands of years to develop and spread.

In general, different people react in different ways to conflict. The classical categories of behavior in conflict are usually defined as:

- Withdraw — avoid conflict

- Compete — use aggression to impose your solution to conflict

- Smooth –yield to the other at the sacrifice of your own feelings

- Compromise — seek a win-win solution that satisfies all parties in conflict

- Collaborate — make an effort to understand the root cause of the conflict and focus on mutual respect over a solution

Which of these approaches is best? Of these reactions, as a leader, you should understand that collaboration is always the best approach — adopting a position of mutual respect will find a solution that can be longer lasting and more acceptable than compromise. It takes a certain amount of creative and critical thinking to use this approach. Your team may not want to behave in this manner, but you should. And you should be direct with them about handling the conflict and inform them of the benefits of collaboration.

Another important approach to conflict is to make sure that it gets resolved at the lowest level of the organization. The more layers of people that get involved in attempting to placate or mitigate the conflict, the less likely it is that a healthy and lasting resolution will be found. Good leaders push back on escalating conflict, encouraging those in conflict to collaborate to find a solution. It saves time and resources and creates a healthier atmosphere overall.

Did you know that when properly managed, conflict can be healthy? As a leader, you need to be able to "mine" for conflict — make sure that potentially controversial ideas are surfaced and resolved in a professional manner. Appropriately surfacing and resolving conflict can build stronger working relationships and teams. You may recall Tuckman's model of the team life cycle — forming, storming, norming, performing, and closing. In the storming stage, leaders are challenged for control, and issues generated can lead to hostility, anger, and unproductive time. Team members need to move past the "I" and understand that it's about the "we". That realization can take time, and as a leader, you need to be able to help.

Organizational conflicts can be much more serious and costly. Resolving workplace and organizational conflict has been estimated to take up to 28 hours per week or a little more than half the work week. Based on that working estimate and average salaries, PSP, Inc., a software company providing tools to enhance organizational performance, has estimated the annual cost of conflict in the US workplace as $359B annually. Studies have shown that fewer than 5% of conflicts start as interpersonal conflict — it is mostly between departments and other work teams, making it a serious issue.

Conflict has real cost associated with it, so as a leader, to avoid wasting time and other resources, you need to have preventive measurements in place and be able to handle the unpreventable. The first step is understanding where conflict originates. I've found over the year that there are four primary sources of conflict in any organization or team:

- Conflicting priorities or too many high priorities
- Lack of communications
- Misunderstandings of urgency
- Disagreements and disputes over technical issues, ranging from requirements to design to testing

Some other sources include:

- Partner and vendor relationships (e.g. selection processes and payments)
- Organizational change (e.g. re-organization, mergers and acquisitions)
- Finances (e.g. budgets and cash controls)
- Ethics (e.g. broken promises, harassment and abuse)

Stop to think for a moment about these additional sources; it's easy to see that the initial four primary sources are what could be considered root causes. For example, an organizational change without communications and buy-in to the change and appropriate priorities for implementation can lead to confusion and conflict. With that in mind, let's take a look at three tools you can use to successfully "mine" for and prevent conflict in your organization:

- Governance processes that provide clarity to the organization or team
- An "egoless" review process that helps to bring out the best ideas

- Active listening as a way to "hear" what the root cause of the conflict really is

Leaders can prevent some conflict or at least contain the severity by putting the right governance processes and procedures in place. Clarity of vision, purpose, plan, and roles and responsibilities are essential elements. Having these in place means that all decisions, recommendations, and actions that might lead to conflict can be reasonably compared to expectations. This has to be done at a high level — micromanagement will only cause more conflict.

Clarity usually starts with strategic planning — a process an organization will use to set its direction through the formation of a mission and vision. It's also important for the organization to identify the behaviors that are acceptable and unacceptable. At the highest levels, this again comes from the ability to compare to organizational norms, usually set through documents such as a code of professional conduct and ethics. Departments and work teams should develop their own "team contracts" or "team operating agreements". By ensuring your teams are setting norms and ground rules, you're empowering all to contribute to what is acceptable and to self-manage the unacceptable. Avoiding blame, we need to focus on the issues, rather than the people.

Every organization needs to make decisions about priorities, urgencies, and "technical" matters specific to their industry and work. All decisions and major documents such as requirements, analysis, and design can benefit from a review conducted in a manner which reduces conflict, enforces respect, and gets the best thinking to be applied constructively. I've found the following "egoless review" process outlined here can help arrive at the right decisions, with as much buy-in as possible, with team involvement including the best ideas possible, and with some natural barriers that checking egos during the deliberations:

- For any decision or document to be reviewed, distribute it up to five business days in advance (time depending on the amount of material) along with a meeting invitation.

- The meeting agenda should cover an hour (again depending on the amount of material — if substantially more than an hour is required, schedule multiple meetings) with the following items:

  - Introduction to the document by the author (5-10 minutes)

  - General comments about the document by reviewers (5-10 minutes)

  - A section-by-section or page-by-page walk through for reviewers to raise issues (30-45 minutes)

  - A summary of the issues by the scribe or facilitator (5-10 minutes)

  - A simple majority decision on next steps (5-10 minutes)

- Critical ground rules for the meeting should include:

  - We collect issues and their facts, let the author take responsibility for the next steps outside of the meeting.

  - Simple spelling, grammar, and formatting issues should not be raised in the meeting — they should be passed privately to the author before or after the meeting.

  - The collective review team recommends an action at the end, normally one of the following: a) we accept the document "as is" and/or trust the author to make the final updates (no additional meetings required), b) the document is acceptable and we want to review the updates, and c) we don't accept the document and believe major updates are required for the next review.

Based on that final assessment, it is incumbent on the document author to take the next steps to publish or make updates and arrange for the next review.

Now many organizations will argue that they don't have time for this process. However, the time is fairly minimal — an hour or so meeting and an hour or so per reviewer to formulate issues and ideas for improvement. The process encourages decision makers and document authors to "do their homework" and come to the meeting well prepared. The process is as close to "egoless" as possible, and the result is usually better ideas as a result of team effort. Contrast this with 28 hours per week lost to conflict, and the choice is a "no brainer"!

As one final skill, I present "active listening" for your consideration. Active listening is often referred to as "listening with all the senses". I like to think of active listening as getting into GEAR:

- **G**ive verbal responses
- Maintain **e**ye contact
- **A**sk relevant questions
- **R**estate and reframe for understanding

According to Wikipedia, "[Active listening] requires that the listener fully concentrate, understand, respond and then remember what is being said." Figure 1 illustrates a complete model of communications. Let's dissect the definition and model one idea at a time so you will more fully appreciate its important role in conflict resolution.

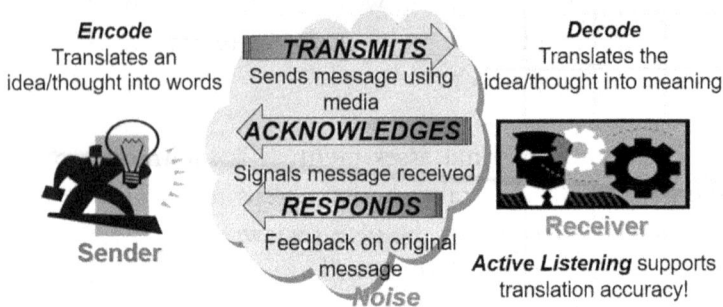

Figure 1: A Model of Communications

Concentrate means that you have focused attention. You're not thinking about what to have for lunch or how much you hate the way the person you are conversing with is dressed — you are freeing your mind from these distracting thoughts and noise of all kinds, physical and mental. Concentration means you will be able to fully hear and interpret everything that is said.

Understanding is about assigning meaning to the words that you heard. You are also interpreting the message free from biases with your concentration. Active listening supports your own translation of words into meaning.

And once you believe you have reached an understanding, you should respond. For a time, this might just be simple head nods and uttered uh-huhs, but when the speaker is finished, you should confirm your understanding through paraphrasing and similar communication techniques. In the event there is a lot of negativity in the message, a technique called "re-framing" can be used to paraphrase, but with the negativity removed. If someone says, "that's a stupid idea", a re-framed response might be "so you don't believe that course of action will yield the best results?"

Active listening is a great skill to learn for many reasons, and it can be used in many contexts (all of which may include conflict) including:

- Requirements gathering
- Client meetings
- Dealing with family and friends
- Consulting

To fully practice active listening also requires a high degree of self-awareness, an important trait you will need as a leader. This means you need to be aware of and set aside feelings:

- Prejudice — feelings of bias you may have toward people and situations

- Discomfort — uncomfortable feelings about the subject matter of the discussion

- Relationships — how you relate to any people that are part of the discussion

- Environment — the physical environment the discussion is taking place in

- Judging — any preconceived notions you may have about the topic of discussion as all of these may impair your ability to appropriately translate messages.

Now I'd like to take you one layer deeper to better understand the role of active listening in conflict resolution. While on the surface, conflict may appear to be about technical ideas, conflict is very often generated by the deeper wants and needs (e.g. a need for respect, a need to maintain a technical position). During a dialog with active listening, if you listen closely enough, test your understanding, and ask clarifying questions, you will be able to uncover those hidden wants and needs.

When practicing active listening, open ended questions will help draw out these hidden needs. Questions like, "How would you like things to be different?", invite the speaker to articulate their vision for a solution. In general, almost any question that helps pinpoint the solution is good, however if the conflict is at an intense emotional level, it is best that you avoid asking "why" questions as this allows speakers to go back to the past and re-live a bad experience. Active listening should uncover positive, current and future needs.

Once these hidden wants and needs have surfaced, now you can begin to craft options for resolving conflict, all the while continuing to practice active listening. Additional open discussion and brainstorming can be used to work out the details. State the core issue as a "how" problem then share and discuss ideas.

Will you unite or divide? As a leader, the choice is yours. When conflict happens, you need to address it quickly. Otherwise it can spread and polarize your leaders and team members quickly. They begin to "take sides" and the conflict spreads. When conflict spreads, it becomes costlier and more difficult to contain and resolve.

Conflict can be an opportunity. Divergent opinions are valuable to leaders and should be considered. But we want to review them in controlled circumstances, not under battle conditions! Without conflict management skills, leaders will see their teams become divided and fail. By successfully navigating conflict, leaders can unify teams and organizations and see conflict as an opportunity to collaborate, grow, and succeed.

References and Readings

"Leading at a higher level: Blanchard on how to be a high-performing leader" by Kenneth Blanchard

"The speed of trust: why trust is the ultimate determinate of success or failure in your relationships, career and life" by Stephen M. R. Covey

"Why motivating people doesn't work and what does: the new science of leading, energizing, and engaging" by Susan Fowler

"The Five Dysfunctions of a Team. New York" by Patrick M. Lencioni

"Crucial confrontations: tools for resolving broken promises" by Kerry Patterson, Joseph Grenny, Ron McMillan, and Al Switzler

Notes:

_____
_____
_____
_____
_____

ABOUT THE AUTHOR
RAY FROHNHOEFER, MBA, PMP, CCP

Ray is the Managing Partner of Precise Projects Consulting Group, LLC (PPC Group, LLC), as well as an instructor and mentor at several Southern California learning institutions, including California Southern University and UCSD Extension. Through PPC Group, LLC, Ray offers project management training, consulting, and books to help organizations succeed through continuous improvement and application of best practices.

Ray has 35+ years of project, program, and portfolio management experience, working with organizations such as General Electric Information Services, Siebel Systems, and Verizon Wireless. For growing organizations that want to improve performance and grow, Ray is a hands-on executive with strong project, program, and portfolio management skills, a methodologist, and a creative inventor and entrepreneur. His mission: improve the practice of project, program, and portfolio management in multiple industries and organizations.

His key leadership qualities have enabled Ray to save companies millions of dollars by his ability to efficiently make complex decisions, solve complex problems, and get projects and programs done, even under pressure. He wants to be a change agent for your project success.

Ray's project management strengths include planning, development of innovative methodologies, conflict resolution, and software implementation management.

Contact Information:

PPC Group, LLC
439 West Washington Avenue Unit 405
Escondido CA 92025

Website: http://ppcgroup.us

Phone: 1.760.685.2197

5

EMOTIONAL INTELLIGENCE: THE MISSING LINK IN PROJECT DYNAMICS

Geoff Crane

In 1995, Daniel Goleman published his popular book, *Emotional Intelligence*, capturing the world's attention. The business community latched on to Goleman's opus, fascinated by its implications for hiring, training and business improvements. Indeed, *Time Magazine* hailed Goleman's work as one of the twenty-five most influential business management books of all time. As the popularity of the domain exploded, so too has the volume of serious literature intent on exploring its value in predicting occupational success, from a variety of perspectives.

Emotions, however, have been around as long as humans have walked the earth. So why, then, has emotional intelligence (EI) suddenly become so important to the working world? What is EI and what makes it distinct from other, more well-known measures of performance? In particular, why should EI matter to you, the project professional? In this chapter, we will explore the answers to all of these questions and offer some helpful techniques to improve your EI as you work through your next project.

WHAT IS EI?

The idea of emotional intelligence is not new and has deep roots in academic literature. Well over a century ago, Charles Darwin (1872) spoke of the *adaptive utility of emotions*, drawing connections between evolution and emotional expression. Fifty years later, Edward Thorndike (1920) would describe the concept of *social intelligence* as "the ability to understand and manage men and women to act wisely in human relations". More recently, Howard Gardner (1983) proposed his *theory of multiple intelligences* which included self-awareness and interpersonal skills not traditionally associated with cognitive intelligence.

While scientists generally recognize that humans possess mental abilities that traditional measures of intelligence (like IQ) can't touch, quantifying these skills has proven difficult. Many researchers have risen to the challenge, however, and one model in particular has emerged that enjoys wide consensus in the industry. EI, it suggests, is a constellation of skills and abilities that represents a cross-section of social, emotional and motivational attributes. Arguably the most popular representation of this model is the Bar-On *Emotional Quotient Inventory* (1997). This assessment decomposes EI into four different dimensions. They are: intrapersonal abilities, interpersonal abilities, adaptability and stress management. Each one of these skill groups overlaps with the others as per the diagram below.

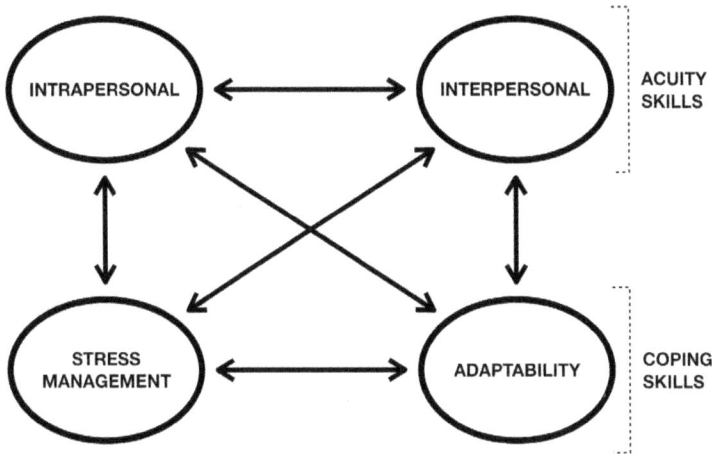

For a variety of genetic and environmental reasons, each person possesses different levels of each of these skills and will use them for different reasons and in different ways. Because these dimensions exist in a personality-like space, measurement of this EI model results in unique profiles for each individual. However, groups of people can share certain traits. Project managers, for example, tend to have similar experiences around planning, negotiation, management of scarce resources and more that help give shape to their overall EI. What follows is a breakdown of the above four dimensions presented in a project management context.

Interpersonal Skills. As the name suggests, this cluster of abilities involves activities associated with the emotions of other people. Project professionals would leverage these skills during negotiations with vendors, managing team members and working with stakeholders. Individuals high in interpersonal functioning would be able to easily sell ideas and get buy-in from those around them. Adept at finding common ground and developing non-zero-sum solutions where everybody wins, those with strong interpersonal skills would present empathy at the right times and find the easiest path through emotional challenges with others.

Adaptability Skills. These talents have to do with a project professional's ability to process and tolerate change. Essentially the cognitive side of coping, individuals high in this area would be excellent decision makers, be able to think laterally and have a firm grasp of reality even under pressure. Adaptable project managers would rarely let strong emotions overcome their ability to think rationally—others would look to their leadership during times of crisis.

Stress Management Skills. This group of abilities represents the physiological side of coping. Central here are bodily regulation of stress and management of impulses. Project professionals who score highly in this area would be able to control inappropriate urges and not make rash decisions without first thinking them through. These individuals will place a priority on taking good physical care of themselves so that they have the resources to deal with the effects that their stressful careers have on their bodies.

Intrapersonal Skills. Finally, this cluster of skills catalogues an individual's potential for self-awareness and the ability to look inward. Project workers with high intrapersonal scores would have no problem setting boundaries for themselves or for their projects. Indeed, when stakeholders attempt to push the limits of their authority, project managers with strong intrapersonal skills would respectfully but firmly maintain scope control. Highly self-reflective, these individuals would understand the consequences of their actions and promptly recognize red flags that suggest their project is in jeopardy.

It is unlikely that even the most skilled project manager will excel in all of the above areas. Everyone has areas for improvement. However, just as analytical skills improve with exposure to project work, so too do the skills we associate with EI. Simply working in the project space can help build your sense of perceived competence and mastery of discipline-specific emotional and social skills. It might, however, sometimes be a bumpy ride.

WHAT EI IS NOT

As buzzwords enter popular consciousness, their definitions often get twisted around as people try to interpret them outside of their original context. EI is no exception to this phenomenon and frequent public discourse around the topic has resulted in misconceptions regarding its definition. The following are some common EI myths debunked:

EI is not about "being nice". Indeed, there are many times in our lives when we have to "park our empathy" to deal with a particular situation. One would not, for example, say "that's okay" to an employee who has defied a supervisor, or stop to make sure nobody's feelings are hurt during a fire alarm. An emotionally intelligent individual would be able to recognize occasions where an empathetic response would be inappropriate and would instead use emotional information to guide their decision-making process.

EI is not about giving free reign to emotions. Regardless of circumstance, it is not always appropriate to express our feelings, and some situations even call for disingenuousness. A funeral director, for example, would be ill-advised to laugh or tell jokes at work even if they found something funny. A trading floor manager, however, might need to leverage humor to help his or her staff maintain perspective during a crisis. Those with high levels of EI would immediately recognize the time and place for certain emotional expressions and comport themselves accordingly.

EI is not fixed. Because of the similarity in names, many people confuse cognitive intelligence, which remains fairly stable over a person's life, with EI. This, however, is a misnomer. EI tends to improve with every challenge we survive. "That which doesn't kill you makes you stronger," is an old adage that reflects this process. Each time we overcome difficult situations, we develop emotional and social strategies to deal with that situation the next time it occurs. This is the essence of emotional maturity and it never stops improving. You will be your most emotionally intelligent on your deathbed!

WHY SHOULD PROJECT MANAGERS WORRY ABOUT EMOTIONAL INTELLIGENCE?

Everybody struggles with emotional and social challenges, and project professionals are no exception. There are certain issues, however, that tend to crop up with fair frequency for those who work in the project space. This is not to say that other professions don't experience these challenges; just that project workers tend to experience them more. What follows is a list of three important vulnerability factors that can influence a project manager's ability to perform their work and maintain a certain level of mental health.

Insufficient Stress Reduction. Project work is stressful, and opportunities for stress management can change from one project to the next depending on the nature of higher-order organizational relationships. Client companies, for example, don't need to provide any stress management opportunities to project workers who are not their direct employees. Professional service firms are in a position to offer loose commitments to those staff whom they contract out; however, these commitments tend to be ephemeral since the employee performs their duties elsewhere. Self-employed professionals have no such shelter.

Organizational commitment to the employee should not be underestimated. Beyond straight compensation (e.g. benefits, salary, etc.), companies traditionally offer their permanent employees psychological protections not always available along the project management pathway. Vacation time, for example, is a feature built-in to most full-time employment that allows employees to recuperate after periods of intense work. Contract and professional service workers often neglect these rest periods either because their organization measures them on billable uptime, or because they need to focus on finding their next project. Indeed, many project professionals recognize the lack of suitable recuperation as a major source of stress.

Identity Reconstruction. Exhaustion is not the only source of stress to a project worker. Incumbents also need to have a sense of who they are within an occupational context. As workers move from one job to the next, they have no opportunity to develop a stable identity within their company. To make matters worse, the transitory nature of their work often forces individuals to rebuild their identity in a manner that is consistent with their new community—every time they shift jobs. The consequences of continuous reconfiguration of one's identity can be harmful. According to Beech (2011), contract workers often get treated like outsiders in the workplace. As a result, many project professionals find themselves making repeated, frustrated attempts to fit in. The longer these attempts remain unsuccessful, the more likely these individuals will be to develop negative dispositions towards their colleagues, company and ultimately, themselves.

Disengagement. As a worker's sense of self deteriorates, it is easy to imagine that their decision-making abilities may become compromised. In 2014, Reevy and Deason recognized that university faculty who worked in contract positions might feel isolated from their tenured counterparts. Not surprisingly, their respondents overwhelmingly identified the precariousness of their employment as the single greatest stressor in their professional experience. The team noted that their results were consistent with earlier research suggesting that contract work is itself a source of stress. Most importantly, they noted that 50% of their sample was especially at risk for negative health outcomes. A review of their regression matrix showed that this finding may be a direct consequence of outlook: in general, the longer participants worked in a temporary capacity, the more likely they were to adopt disengagement coping mechanisms as a way to deal with their predicament. This cluster of strategies includes denial, occupational disengagement ("giving up") and substance abuse.

The complex nature of project work may also influence the decision-making paradigms of its practitioners. Sennett (1998) argues that "character corrosion" is becoming an important hallmark of project-based work. He contends that the flexibility a project environment demands often separates the people who work within it. Workers who are more adaptable tend to form more secure relationships with their colleagues than those who have trouble with new ideas. As a result, professionals with a more rigid outlook towards their project may find themselves increasingly vulnerable to the vagaries of their position. Further, project-based work is susceptible to the legal dilemma known as "the moral hazard". This occurs when those paying for a project (or paying the salary of a worker on that project) have objectives that do not align with the objectives of the project itself. This phenomenon can place undue pressure on workers to behave in unethical ways so as to placate those controlling their income.

While the above risks in no way account for the breadth of potential derailments to a project professional's career, one can infer that, in combination, they comprise an important threat to success. To be effective, then, project workers should be able to: 1) manage the stress inherent in a job devoid of the usual securities, 2) adapt to the vagaries of a career spent in transition, and 3) retain their moral compass in the face of multiple, conflicting stakeholder demands. For purposes of discussion, we will label this collection of attributes as "resilience". According to the foregoing, one would expect project managers with poor resilience to struggle. Those with poor adaptability, for example, may find themselves unable to let go of old ways of working (which new employers may find undesirable). Workers unable to cope with stress, or who find themselves making poor decisions under pressure may develop poor reputations. Since project professionals often shift jobs even while working for the same employer, cues to deficiencies in resilience may appear in the frequency and duration of these transitions. In other words, professionals with high resilience should move from project to project with a minimum of disruption while workers with poor resilience should struggle through each break, with longer and more frequent gaps than highly resilient professionals.

Ways to improve EI

Fortunately, as mentioned earlier, EI is highly malleable. With attention and work, anyone can set themselves up for success with significant improvements to their emotional and social intelligence. The following are just a few tips to help build confidence and performance in each of the four EI domains.

Interpersonal Improvements. Empathy is central to so many tasks that a project manager needs to perform. Negotiation, selling ideas, influence without authority and more…they all begin with the ability to empathize and understand the position of another. The FBI has long recognized the importance of empathy in driving behaviour changes of people who find themselves on the brink of committing dangerous behaviours. In fact, their Behaviour Change Stairway Model (see diagram) works just as well for hostage negotiators as it does for project managers seeking to drive specific interpersonal outcomes. According to the model, deliberate attention to active listening offers a path to empathy. From there, rapport develops, which can lead to the influence required to effect specific changes in others' behaviour. When used effectively, project professionals can substantially improve their interpersonal skills.

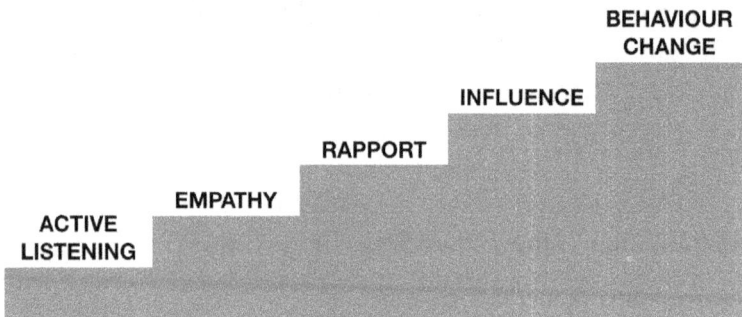

Adaptability Improvements. When you know that a particular upcoming event is likely to be stressful (e.g., terminating a team member, placating an angry stakeholder), you can improve your performance by planning the event out ahead of time. Think through possible emotions that could emerge during such situations and make decisions about how you will handle them if they arise. How should you best respond, for example, to a display of anger? Sadness? Contempt? Should your behaviour change depend on your seniority against the person making the display? Your answers to these questions should address more than just your own feelings. We often think through immediate consequences of our actions and decisions but seldom think two, three or four steps beyond them. In the face of someone's hostility, tears or bitterness, what is likely to happen if you take a firm position? What would happen after that? And after that?

Stress Management Improvements. As our world becomes more and more connected it becomes increasingly difficult to disengage from it. This, however, is precisely what we need to be able to develop personal resilience. We can no longer expect to just switch off personal electronic devices during scheduled downtimes and find relaxation. Last minute communications can create stress long after the distracting technology has been put away. Successful disengagement from stressful stimuli requires planning out a schedule. This schedule should include "winding down" periods that allow you to mentally prepare to relax. Unwinding is a crucial step in the process of disconnection and provides the opportunity to put stressors in their proper perspective. Maintaining a healthy lifestyle and making time for technology-free social activities can help prevent stress from becoming chronic.

Intrapersonal Improvements. Self-awareness is perhaps the most challenging of the emotional and social skill families to improve because it requires a substantial amount of introspection. In general, it is good practice to spend at least a part of each day thinking over your most recent experiences and trying to articulate how you feel about them. One technique that has withstood the test of time is journaling. Keep a diary handy and document your day before you go to bed. Pay particular attention to the feelings you had toward your colleagues, your work, and the decisions you made over the course of the day. Did you wish you had handled something differently? How might you do it next time? If you find it challenging to think about what to write, you may find it helpful to plan out a series of journaling prompts to start your thoughts flowing. Busy millennials have found that "bullet journals" make for an easy variation on this technique—the Internet abounds with *BuJo* templates that make this experience easy and fun.

No matter where you find yourself in your project management journey, it's important to recognize that emotional and social skills play a crucial part of your ability to deliver. This chapter only scratches the surface of the ways in which you can improve them. As your career continues to unfold, you will find new strategic pathways to map and explore. Along the way, I wish you the very best of success.

NOTES:

_____

_____

_____

ABOUT THE AUTHOR
GEOFF CRANE

A. Geoffrey "Geoff" Crane is a Canadian public speaker, researcher and entrepreneur. As a pioneer in the field of motivational intelligence, he has written numerous articles on the importance of emotional and social skills in the workforce. Well-versed in the changing demands of today's project-based work environments, Geoff spends his days helping leaders design and build a balanced repertoire of soft skills to help them achieve what matters most.

As with a lot of young professionals, when Geoff began his career he had little experience to draw from. His job as a project manager began almost accidentally — it was a new and poorly defined role within the business world and he was unwittingly thrown into it. Feeling lost, he was forced to navigate on his own through the uncertainty of managing large-scale projects and the interpersonal conflicts that arose between competing stakeholders.

Eventually, these difficulties led to burnout and he was laid off around the 2008 financial crisis. In the aftermath while unsuccessfully trying to find work, Geoff realized his passions needed rethinking and he decided to return to academia. Focusing on psychology, his studies centered on interpersonal relationships in the workplace, which led to the development of an emotional intelligence training program. With Geoff's personal story very much a part of the inspiration and essence of the training programs he developed, Adaptimist Insights was born.

Business Address:

Adaptimist Insights
P. O. Box 30063
RPO Chemong Road
Peterborough, Ontario
CANADA K9H 7R4

Telephone:+1-705-772-2300

E-mail: geoff.crane@adaptimist.com

Website: http://adaptimist.com

6

EXERCISING INFLUENCE
WITHOUT AUTHORITY

Tony Adams

Ask people in your workplace whether they can influence others in their current role and count the responses. Most will say something like:

- "I'm just a worker, I don't have any authority."

- "Only my boss has the power to influence what happens here."

Do you hear the key words coming through?

Power. Authority. Influence.

There's a common thread linking these three words together — the notion that you need authority or power, before you can influence others.

Yet take a look around your community and you can see people making a difference and influencing others every day. How does that happen? How do people exercise influence in their daily lives, when they are just like us — doing the best they can, without any real authority?

INFLUENCING MATTERS

Strip it all down and influencing is simply about *deepening our relationships and commitment to the end result.*

It's about building relationships, finding common ground, understanding what your audience is looking for and finding ways to guide them towards help you.

- Help your teams and stakeholders feel committed to the project goal

- Helping people see why your project matters, so that they willingly commit time, expertise and resources to help you get there

WHY YOU SHOULD BE INFLUENCING

Your ability to build relationships with your clients, team members and partners, and receive their commitment to helping you sits at the core of your effectiveness as a Project Leader.

- You need to influence your team members to execute your work plan

- You need to influence your Sponsor so that he or she champions your issue, problem, constraint or opportunity

- You need to influence your senior stakeholders, partners and vendors so they offer their expertise and support, when you need them most

How Can We Influence Others?

How can you, as a Project Leader, exercise influence in your workplace, when you have little formal authority?

If we take the time to understand the behavior of the people across our project, we can actively steer discussions and shape our key decisions.

Robert Cialdini's research into social psychology helps us understand how to use human behavioral patterns to influence the behavior of others. Cialdini's seminal work ("Influence: The Psychology of Persuasion," 1984) says that to exercise influence, we need to use a combination of 6 important principles.

Principle 1 - Reciprocity

If people receive a gift or service, they will generally want to give something back in return.

If someone does you a favor, you feel obliged to reciprocate.

If your work colleague buys you a coffee, it feels like the right thing to pay for the next one.

*If your request for help is **preceded by an unexpected gift**, the recipient is more likely to offer support in return. People are wired this way. One good turn deserves another.*

Cialdini used the example of the 1985 Mexican earthquake. Ethiopia, in the midst of a disastrous famine and crushing internal strife, donated generously to Mexico's recovery process. Why? If you follow the trail of Ethiopia - Mexico relations back to 1935, Mexico was one of only 5 countries in the League of Nations to denounce the Italian invasion and occupation in 1935. That event was the trigger for the next 50 years of reciprocal friendship. One good turn deserves another.

The key to using the Reciprocity Principle to influence others is to reach out to the other person early and offer something that is both meaningful and unexpected.

Case Study
Joe needed expert help to develop training materials for his upcoming product launch. Elizabeth wanted to help but didn't have anyone available until well beyond the launch date.

Understanding Elizabeth's predicament, Joe offered to create the training outline, storyboards and raw content, in formats that made Elizabeth's job much easier.

This was simple for his team, while at the same time, a huge help for Elizabeth. In return, Elizabeth was able to re-prioritize her remaining work and help to Joe meet his launch date.

Putting This Principle into Practice
Talk with each of your stream leaders and understand their top three requirements before they can support your work. Deliver the top priority within 2 days.

Buy your Sponsor a coffee and talk about how you can make the most immediate difference to his business. Provide a plan to deliver early, targeted value.

Principle 2 - Scarcity
People want more of what they can't have.

When a long running theatre production releases final tickets and announces the end of its season, we often see a renewed spike in sales. Yet nothing has changed about the production. Same cast, same story. If it's been running a long time, chances are that you're familiar with it - you've read reviews, maybe even know a few people who have been to see it.

Simply, the tickets become a scarce commodity and people don't want to miss out.

> *We want more of what we can't have; **things are more valuable when they become scarce**, or when we risk missing out on the unique value that they bring.*

Influencing others through the Scarcity Principle is about letting people see what they miss out on if they don't use your idea or product. More than just telling people why your solution is the best, you also need to spell out the unique value that they stand to lose if they don't consider your proposition.

Case Study

Mary needed to recruit 2 more analysts onto her project team to complete her product development and testing.

Understanding that budgets were tight, Mary pitched her case around the market and revenue opportunities that would be realized if the product was launched early.

Her key message became "by investing $5,000 in two additional analysts now, we will get Product ABC to market in time for the North American sales convention which means we can book additional sales of $50,000. Work with us now, and we can help you get that additional revenue this financial year."

Putting This Principle into Practice

Work with your Product Managers to understand the sales pipeline — when will products be launched and what revenue is forecast. Blend this roadmap into your project plan so that you have a clear view of when those value opportunities arise.

Talk to your Sponsor and understand her top product priorities. Which products will deliver the greatest benefit to her business? Know what it means to the Business bottom line to have these products delivered early or late.

Principle 3 — Authority

Given a question and a choice of two people to answer, people will almost always lean towards the person whom they regard as the credible, knowledgeable expert.

Want people to listen to you? You need to make it crystal clear that you and your team are "credible" and "knowledgeable" experts, and that your words carry weight and can be trusted.

Your team wants to know that you understand the space they are working in.

Your stakeholders want to know that you understand how their big issues will affect their business and can speak with clarity about how your Project will respond.

People lean towards authority figures; you need to make it clear that your words carry weight and can be trusted.

Using the Authority Principle to influence decisions is about showing the Business that you understand their issues and lead a highly skilled team that can deliver the right solution.

Case Study
Before meeting his new Project Sponsor for the first time, Blair did some research.

He knew that Helen wanted to know that she had the right team in place, with a Project Manager who was a trusted, knowledgeable voice in this area.

Blair took time before the meeting to compile a briefing note covering 5 current industry issues and trends, together with how they affected Helen's business. He made sure that key knowledge areas were prominently displayed on his LinkedIn, Yammer and other corporate profiles, and reinforced his team's authority by flagging each member's primary area of expertise.

When he met with Helen, Blair was able to speak confidently about hot-button issues, including how they would affect her business and how the Project would respond.

Helen immediately felt confident that she had the right Project Manager in place, and that Blair's team understood the issues that mattered most to her.

Putting This Principle into Practice
Maintain a Briefing Note (your "30 second elevator pitch") that covers your organization's critical market issues and opportunities - including how your project will support the business strategy. Make sure that every senior stakeholder receives a copy.

Build a simple Executive Summary to share your team's story

- Who is in your team - put faces to names, talk about their experience, formal qualifications and notable achievements

- The team's Top 5 areas of expertise, experience and high-value outcomes

- What challenges the team has faced and how they have responded

Principle 4 - Commitment (and Consistency)
People want to show consistent attitudes and behaviors that reflect their personal values and priorities. We present ourselves in a way that reflects how we see ourselves.

To do this, we make small commitments everyday — decisions and actions that we repeat over time.

We attend our church each week because the pastor's message reflects our values.

We join football training with our local team because we want to be part of something larger than ourselves.

When we do this consistently, we show a pattern of behavior that shapes the way people see us.

> ***When making decisions***, *we make commitments that reflect our values and priorities; over time, these provide a consistent pattern of behavior - our personal Calling Card.*

Using the Commitment (and Consistency) Principle to influence others is about looking at your stakeholder's "calling card", identifying their visible, active commitments that are repeated consistently over time, and then blending them into your planning and negotiations.

Case Study
Paul was planning the rollout of a new product across the company. With clients already showing interest, he needed to work out the best way to deploy the product and gain his Project Board's support.

Paul's first step was to spend time with the Project Office to understand how previous products had been delivered. This understanding helped him quickly find the funding and deployment approach that best resonated with his Sponsor.

Putting This Principle into Practice
Talk to your critical stakeholders and understand how they like to see change delivered into their business. What approach has worked for them in the past? Do they want to continue that approach with your project?

Does your Sponsor have a history of funding pilot deployments, before rolling out more broadly across the company? If so, then help him see how this approach could work for your Project.

Do your team members have regular family or other commitments that are important to them? Spend some time understanding what they are and how they can be blended into your team planning.

Principle 5 - Liking
People are more likely to offer support or assistance if they know and respect the other person.

We like to offer our support to someone who connects with us somehow - who pays us a compliment, shares the same values and priorities, and is working towards mutual goals.

We're more likely to be influenced by the people
whom we like.

Using the Liking Principle to exercise influence is about looking for areas of similarity, common values or interests that you share with others and taking the time to make a personal connection around those shared values before you get down to business.

Case Study
Roxanne was ready to start detailed planning with the building contractor on her office fit-out project. With contracts signed and deadlines looming, Roxanne needed to quickly form a plan that had buy-in and support from everyone involved. To break the ice and kick start a collaborative working environment, she pulled everyone together for two kick-off lunches prior to the planning workshops. Using pizza and some friendly conversation to help set the scene for the work to follow, the team got to know each other a little better, find shared interests and create important early connections.

This positive energy followed through into the workshops and with team members connecting through shared interests and familiarity, Roxanne quickly built a plan that had the support of everyone involved.

Putting This Principle into Practice
Catch up with each of your senior stakeholders over coffee and take the time to talk about things that matter to them. Guide the conversation gently, and let the other person speak freely. Remember, this is not a conversation that you need to dominate - it's all about active listening and observing. Notice their body language and idioms. Listen to what they are saying and find the areas of common interest.

Use what you learn from these coffee chats to shape the way that you engage with each of your stakeholders.

Principle 6 — Consensus

If we are uncertain about something, we look to the actions of others for validation or consensus. Running with the herd — it's a universal, primal instinct.

Think about when you want to visit a new restaurant. More and more, we jump online to read reviews and find out what others have said, looking for a consensus opinion to give us certainty.

> When we are not sure about something, we watch what others are doing and look for validation or **consensus** to see if something is OK or not.

The Consensus Principle helps us to influence decisions by pointing out the weight of numbers behind our preferred approach. Use it to make your audience feel good about supporting your approach, by highlighting how other companies, clients or teams have used it and how it has helped them.

Case Study

Eric knew that his Steering Committee would respond to his funding proposal with a range of conflicting opinions that would need to be addressed.

Rather than get bogged down in arguments during his presentation, Eric took time beforehand to brief each Committee member and help them reach a consensus position.

This meant that when he pitched his presentation, it reflected the views of all members and had their in-principle support. Eric was able to use the presentation to quickly reaffirm the prior agreement and reinforce his authority by shaping and locking in the consensus position.

Putting This Principle into Practice
There's nothing quite as important to your project success as making sure that you have the support of your key decision makers.

Understand who these people are. Invest time with them - early and often, to patiently build a consensus position around each of your critical decisions.

What does this mean for Project Leaders?
Project Influence is a long game and there are no shortcuts.

You can certainly improve your ability to influence, but you need to be prepared to invest real time and effort in understanding and applying each of these principles.

SUGGESTED READING

"Influence: The Psychology of Persuasion" by Robert Cialdini, PhD

NOTES:

_____
_____
_____
_____
_____

ABOUT THE AUTHOR
TONY ADAMS

Tony Adams is a Program Leadership Professional, with 25 years of experience as a Consultant, Practitioner, Enabler, Change Agent, Writer and Mentor.

Based in Melbourne Australia, Tony works with companies from around the world, leading complex, innovative change programs that shape the way their users live and work.

Tony's passion is Social Program Leadership — blending traditional project management practices and disciplines with personal communication and technology to help teams engage quickly, connect personally, think creatively, collaborate and drive real, immediate and transformational changes.

Tony is a certified Project Management Professional (PMP) through the Project Management Institute. He earned a Bachelor of Business (Economics and Finance) degree from RMIT University. He also holds a Master of Project Management degree (majoring in Leadership) from the University of Southern Queensland, and is currently studying for a Master in Project Management degree at Monash University.

Contact Information:

Tony Adams

Melbourne, Australia

+614 0786 3600

tonyadamspm.com

7

LEADERS LISTEN!

Todd C. Williams

Leadership and listening are inseparable. The first step in conducting a meaningful conversation on this relationship requires understanding key leadership traits. This builds the foundation for understanding how the two are related. In addition, it points out the role of the leader in creating and listening culture and asking the right questions.

LEADERSHIP BASICS

Leadership is one of the most written about topics. You can learn to be a leader; however, it is mostly an art and no class or book will give you what you need to be a good leader. Some people have the genetics, intuition, or childhood experiences to make them naturally good leaders. The rest of us need lots of introspection, advice, success, and lots of practice. Not all leaders are good in every situation. Some of us can lead companies, others can lead projects, some can lead volunteers, and other people seem to have the ability to lead anyone. Some people do not want to lead and others cannot. There are a few who try and fail and there are some people who never realize they have failed at leading. There is no set formula. The opening story describes a special situation that requires a mix of leadership strategies that change over time.

Many "leaders" get that label from their position in the hierarchy of the organization. It may be that they are elected to be on a leadership council of a professional organization or they are promoted due to superlative professional performance. These are leaders who are placed into a role and often have no training on what it really takes to be a leader. We have all suffered under some of those reigns.

Leadership, however, is not exclusive to the people at the top of an organization. In fact, many top executives are dismal leaders. Leaders are needed throughout the organization. We need leaders for divisions, departments, initiatives, projects, customers, clients, and individual contributors. Since we have trouble getting good leaders to run our governments and companies, we have even more difficulty finding people with leadership skills to work at all levels within our organizations.

If the goal is to complete projects successfully that deliver value to the customer, then leaders are required throughout the hierarchy—from the executive to the individual contributor. Too often, when we hire people, we overlook selecting them on their leadership characteristics. Individual contributors—analysts, architects, builders, designers, developers, trainers, and testers—collectively meet with the customer more than most other people associated with the project. In the course of doing their jobs, these individuals lead the customer toward a solution that the customer *needs* versus *wants* and have the technical expertise to translate those wants, needs, and desires into a set of deliverables that a project team can create. This process is "leading the customer through the process of discovery" (a technique discussed later in this chapter). The operative word is *lead*. If the project team tries to tell customers what they need and not let customers discover that for themselves, customers are less likely to buy in to the idea. Leaders need to listen to their customers. Executives, relationship managers, and even project managers are too far from the end user and detailed knowledge of the solution to influence their decisions. The team's members, who talk on nearly a daily basis with the end user about their problems and potential solutions, are close enough to influence the troops.

ACTIONS OF SUCCESSFUL LEADERS

Traits are the foundation that supports all of our actions—not just for leaders. Reactive tendencies—how we act in given conditions—are a reflection of our traits. These action patterns are difficult, but not impossible, to change. People judge us by these actions. However, as we mold ourselves into better, more effective leaders, our actions will most likely have to change. A person's actions expose their leadership traits and actions cannot lie. Actions, of course, are endless in number so trying to hone in on "actions to identify leaders" would take volumes. Some leaders are out in front of people, often making bold proclamations; others prefer to be further in the background. From experience though, there are five actions that standout over the rest—listening, establishing ownership, fostering dialog and discussion, cultivating a no-fault environment, and selling people on ideas. Three of these reply on listening—listening itself, dialog and discussion, and selling people on ideas.

Listening. By far, the most pronounced action a leader can take is to listen. The combination of listening and leading requires asking the right questions. There are numerous books about listening and active listening for leaders, but the best come from the world of professional sales. People selling high-profile, complex items must have a complete understanding of their customers' needs and the only way they can do that is by asking the right questions to get people to expose their actual issues.

Establishing Ownership. Creating ownership of an idea requires skill and strong persuasive talents. The inputs are to convey why something is being done that allows people to justify changing their beliefs and expectations. The outputs are a sense of urgency, passion, motivation, modified behavior, and finally ownership.

Selling, not Telling. People rarely change by demand. Edict breeds resentment and people revert to their old ways quickly. Therefore, the ability to get people to do something because they truly want to, persuasion, is what enables leadership throughout the organization.

Fostering Dialog and Discussion. The foundational gap that this book identifies is a lack of common understanding. Once a common understanding exists, the organization gets buy-in and alignment and change management becomes easier. The critical action here is dialog and discussion; two very different types of discourse which must be understood by everyone.

Cultivating a No-Fault Environment. Open communication will never happen in an accusatory finger-pointing environment where scapegoats and blame surface when difficulties arise. When people think they or a co-worker will be blamed, discourse stops.

This experience is supported by authors such as Jim Collins, Peter Senge, John Kotter, and Patrick Lencioni. In *Good to Great, Why Some Companies Make the Leap and Other Don't*, Jim Collins identifies four principles for leaders getting the information they require (lead with questions, engage in dialog and debate, conduct blameless autopsies, build "red flag" mechanisms). Likewise, in *The Fifth Discipline: The Art & Practice of the Learning Organization*, Senge spends nearly a chapter clarifying the use of dialog versus discussion. Lencioni devotes an entire book (*Getting Naked: A Business Fable about*

Shedding the Three Fears That Sabotage Client Loyalty) to asking the "dumb" questions to lead customers to the right solution.

Listening

A speaker at a recent conference asked the well-dressed audience, "When is the best time to listen?" As with most presenters' questions, there was a host of blank stares, a few people rustled in their seats, and the remainder diverted their eyes to their laps as if a sudden important message had appeared on their tablet or phone. After a pregnant pause the answer came, "When someone is talking." A relieved, yet embarrassed chuckle floated among the suit-clad attendees. The advice is a good start; however, listening entails significantly more effort. The most important action of any leader is listening. Listening is the cornerstone of every decision. The single most important trait of an executive sponsor is listening to the issues, retaining the salient points, and relaying the story back to the critical stakeholders. The traits that make listening effective are being aware, empathetic, and decisive. Listening allows you to understand the people and situations at the core of making good decisions and setting priorities properly.

Listening Is Learning. Fundamental to listening is the concept of learning. If you are not trying to learn something from people speaking, you are not listening. By doing this, you are treating people as if they are an object. Use the same traits when listening as you do when you are learning something. You may repeat what you hear, ask for clarification, or take notes. Taking notes may seem like overkill for many conversations and is inappropriate when people are revealing deeply personal issues; however, writing down what someone says is complimentary to the speaker. Few things make people feel better than having their thoughts being important enough to archive.

Shortly after the turn of the century, I was working for a dot-com that had its first large delivery in Taiwan. The team was the usual male composite, but through the turmoil of a forming company, people fighting for titles, others wrestling to show up the next guy, and the stress of long stints aboard, the team suddenly changed and I found myself working and traveling with a core team of three women and myself. One was my boss. I had worked for numerous women in the past, but none had ever been on the road. The difference became apparent immediately when we all met in the business class lounge waiting for our flight to Seattle out of Taipei. The four of us sat around a table sipping on our beverage of choice trying not to think about the dozen-hour flight that was ahead. One of my team members mentioned a situation with her spouse before we had left and the other two women each asked questions exploring more about her situation. I had the presence of mind to sit and listen, although I was eager to throw in a comment about an incident that happened to me that was almost the same, but twice as embarrassing. I instead asked how she got out of the situation. After fifteen minutes or so, everyone had listened and asked questions. Nobody had offered better stories or solutions to our team member's conundrum. She then asked if anyone had any advice. One or two items were rendered and she thanked us. This was the format of the entire trip and the dozen or so to follow during the project.

Sitting on the plane, I juxtaposed this with what I was used to: Male A saying something happened over the weekend, Male B having something twice as bad as that, Male C having a story even worse, as they took turns playing one-upmanship. Never would we ask how they got out of the situation or how they felt. We would however give the "best advice" ever. Men rarely listened. They seem too busy thinking about "their" story.

The project teams in that engagement showed the same differences. Female led teams were far more cooperative and empathetic; there were less arguments, and happier people (including the customer). Fast forward the clock a decade and I found my company had grown to a nice size of about

14 people—an even mix of employees and contractors. We were working primarily on technology projects in electronics, healthcare, telecom, semiconductor, and the like. Then one day an acquaintance pointed out that only two of the people in the company were male. I had never thought about the mix even though it was completely the opposite of the companies we serviced. I reflected on our hiring process and what I valued when hiring new people. I read a number of books on gender issues in businesses. I wanted to understand the difference. The traits of empathy, humility, accountability, and awareness; the actions of listening, non-aggressiveness, and elimination of blame are part of how our culture raises girls. Studies have shown that women accept their failures while not taking credit for their successes—a common action that is used to describe good leaders. These were heavily weighted traits in how I rated candidates. It is quite the opposite of how we see boys. To be sure, there are women who do not fit this stereotype (no one would ever call Sheryl Sandberg non-aggressive) and there are men who can be empathetic. However, I feel that women (in Western society) are raised with the traits that we look for in good leaders as positive virtues.

Learning Is a Humble Act. Listening with the goal of learning is inherently humble. It says, "You know something I don't and I want to learn it." This is why the leadership trait of being humble is so important. Good leaders are humble. This is part of what makes a leader great. The willingness to listen and learn acknowledges that we do not know everything. Think of people who were great leaders and how they made you feel valued. In a word, they were humble.

You can see how the traits enumerated above are all important as a foundation for being a leader.

Questions Are Critical. By understanding how to ask questions, leaders can get others to buy into concepts without issuing edicts. Questions, though, do more than supply a leader with data to make decisions. They also help the people affected by those decisions understand the basis and buy into the direction. This process of "leading people down the process of discovery" helps develop a common understanding and a sense of ownership and passion around the topic. People feel they are part of a decision.

Action Is Not Necessarily Required. Listening requires participation, not always action. You need to pay attention to *when* to take action. At times, for instance when new to a group or when there has been a major setback, you need to wait to see what action to take with respect to what people are saying. When people raise issues, you need to demonstrate that you heard them through actions not words. The answer may be days or weeks later.

At times, it is not prudent to make wholesale changes, but rather to win the hearts and minds of individuals. Making small changes of a personal nature—getting team members more powerful computers, helping them connect with someone they have had trouble meeting with, or buying them a cinnamon roll for putting in a little extra effort—can demonstrate a new style of leadership and change beliefs and expectations.

There are, however, times when people just want someone to listen. Unfortunately, many of us came up through the ranks of the problem solver, which has conditioned us otherwise. Our lives consist of a continuous stream of puzzles to solve—subordinates presenting problems, children needing help with homework, and myriad of gadgets that need some special knowledge to make them do what we want or what they are supposed to do. We listen, dissect the problem, and take or suggest corrective action. After more than 30 years of marriage, I still struggle with this. More than once my wife has recounted an exasperating situation with one of our children, friends, or work. After dutifully listening to her monologue, I supply a suggestion or solution and it does nothing but increase her frustration. "Would you please stop trying to solve the problem and just listen?" she demands as she retreats to another part of the house. The same thing happens at work. Employees simply stop talking, insincerely acknowledge that they will try your advice, and put more distance between you and them. Our advice may be perfectly valid, but before people will act on it, they have to feel we are listening. It is hard for many of us to listen in a manner that prompts people to talk about issues that matter to them.

Lesson from the Parenting World
The problem with questions is that they can sound like interrogation. Reflect on your childhood, coming home from school, and possibly one of your parents asking you a litany of questions about your day, your lunch, what was fun, what your teacher did, and so forth. It felt like you had just walked into a district attorney's office. Worse than that, most of your feelings were denied. We have all heard some form of this. In fact, you may have used some of these same lines on your children:

> Child: "My teacher hates me."
>
> Parent: "No, he doesn't; I am sure you are fine."
>
> Child: "I had a horrible day. "
>
> Parent: "It could not have been that bad."
>
> Child: "Everyone thinks I am stupid."
>
> Parent: "No they don't; those people are just jealous of your talent."

We do the same thing at work. Not too long ago, I picked up a book by Adele Faberand and Elaine Mazlish titled *How to Talk So Kids Will Listen & Listen So Kids Will Talk*. My intent was not for my professional growth. I wanted to read it because I was feeling a wall go up between my six-year-old adopted daughter, who had just started attending public school, and myself. As I read the book, I started seeing things that happened at work all the time that were shutting down communication. One of their first claims is that we deny people their feelings. For instance, your daughter comes home from school and says her best friend does not like her anymore and you quickly retort trying to soothe her by saying that it is not true and she is making something out of nothing. This shuts down communication. Instead we should respond with an empathetic statement, like "That must make you feel horrible." This gives her an opportunity to open up.

I was at a client site and one of my peers said, "That stakeholder does not like me. I can never get him to come to a meeting." I almost said, "Oh, that's silly. I am sure he is just busy." I chose a different approach and said, "That must be frustrating." The next twenty minutes was a dump of what this stakeholder had done wrong. Had I dismissed the frustration, I would have never heard the reason behind the comment. We talked further and together came up with an action plan to address the stakeholder. A few weeks later all was solved. It took the act of empathetic listening to get the problem exposed. Hearing "frustration" and not a "silly complaint" made it so that we could come up with an action plan. That twenty minutes of being a mentor, probably saved the project a dozen or more hours of frustration.

CONCLUSION

Leaders must listen. Leaders must:

- Create a safe communication environment.
- Indicate when discourse is for making decisions or for brainstorming.
- Frame questions to solicit conversation and not providing direction.

- Build buy-in by leading people through the process of discovery.

Only then will the organization have all the information they need to make the right decisions and succeed.

Recommended Reading

Filling Execution Gaps: How Executives And Project Managers Turn Corporate Strategy Into Successful Projects, by Todd C. Williams

Rescue the Problem Project, A Complete Guide to Identifying, Preventing, and Recovering from Project Failure, by Todd C. Williams

How to Talk So Kids Will Listen & Listen So Kids Will Talk, by Adele Faber & Elaine Mazlish

The Fifth Discipline: The Art & Practice of the Learning Organization, by Peter Senge

Leadership and Self-Deception: Getting Out of the Box, by The Arbinger Institute

ABOUT THE AUTHOR
TODD C. WILLIAMS

A strong comprehensive strategic foundation coupled with operational excellence allows companies to build the capabilities to thrive. Todd C. Williams brings this foundation to your organization. His goal is to improve how companies implement their strategic plans. Utilizing three decades of experience, he helps companies turn their vision into value.

By following the mantra "Strategy, People, Process, and then Technology," he specializes in building success-focused, project-delivery cultures, rescuing projects, and helping organizations drive business value from their strategic plans.

He has worked with all sizes of companies from start-ups to multi-billion enterprises in the US, Far East, and the Middle East. He has working in manufacturing, sales, electronics, healthcare, and automotive. He also works as an expert witness.

Mr. Williams is an internationally acclaimed speaker and trainer doing over 40 presentations, workshops, and custom classes a year throughout the United States, Canada, and European Union. He is a prolific writer contributing to numerous blogs, and a source for Fortune/CNN Money, CIO, CIO Update, ZDNet, Enterprising CIO, IT Business Edge and many other periodicals. Mr. Williams has also authored two books:

- *Filling Execution Gaps: How Executives and Project Managers Turn Corporate Strategy Into Successful Projects* (De Gruyter, 2017)

- *Rescue the Problem Project: A Complete Guide to Identifying, Preventing, and Recovering from Project Failure* (HarperCollins Leadership - AMACOM, 2011)

He is a father of three, a foster parent, and an adoptive father.

Contact Information:

Email: todd.williams@ecaminc.com

Phone: 360-834-7361

Website: http://ecaminc.com

8

SUSTAINED SUCCESS THROUGH NO-NONSENSE NEGOTIATION

Karthik Ramamurthy

WHY IS NEGOTIATION KEY TO LEADERSHIP SUCCESS?

Quick: How often do you negotiate? Did you say monthly, weekly, or daily? In reality, leaders negotiate almost constantly; with customers, bosses, peers, and the teams they lead. Ineffective negotiation can severely affect the probability of your success for your project and your organization.

Are you not entirely comfortable while negotiating? Do you sometimes experience negotiation nightmares? You're not alone. I was in the same situation a few decades ago. I invested time and money in books and training. I repeatedly practiced the techniques I learned whenever I could. Today, I confidently and frequently negotiate favorable results. You can too! Leveraging your innate qualities and building the right skillset and mindset cannot happen overnight. You will need to carefully analyze where you are today, where you want to go, plot your path ahead, and work hard to develop the skills you need.

Key Factors for Negotiating Success

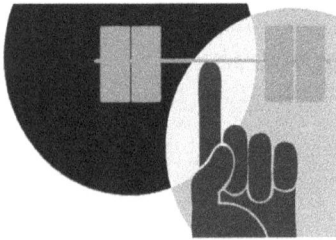

My company frequently conducts "Negotiation Success" workshops for leaders. We carried out deep research into key competencies needed. In carrying out this research, we used the "poll of polls" approach. We consolidated rankings across several published research studies by factoring the number of competencies listed in each study and their ranking within each one. Table A lists these results. Rate yourself: On a scale of one to 10 (low to high), what is your confidence level? This self-rating is valuable; it will help you analyze where you need to invest most time and effort in becoming a great negotiator.

#	Competence/ Quality	Self-Rating	#	Competence/ Quality	Self-Rating
1	Negotiating Skills & Experience		11	Persuasiveness	
2	Communication skills		12	Diligence	
3	Creative Thinking & Flexibility		13	Decisiveness	
4	Relevant Knowledge		14	Sense of humor	
5	Seeing the Big Picture		15	Confidence	
6	Detailed Planning		16	Ambitiousness & Risk Tolerance	
7	Ethical approach		17	Non-egotistic approach	
8	Self-awareness		18	Stamina	
9	Empathy		19	Body Language Basics	
10	Patience		20	Learning from the Past	

Table A: Key factors in successful negotiation

The "Recommended Reading" section at the end of this chapter lists valuable books that can help you improve in areas where you didn't rate yourself highly.

Here's a story which demonstrates the importance of the top 10 competencies.

NEGOTIATION SUCCESS STORY: RAHUL ACHIEVES WIN-WIN RESULTS FOR WINNINGEDGE SOLUTIONS

Rahul was quite anxious as he finished an important call with his boss. He had been asked to head negotiations to finalize the terms for a major Customer Relations Management (CRM) system for WeBuildWell, a mid-sized construction company. In working with WinningEdge Solutions for almost four years, Rahul had successfully negotiated many small and medium deals. However, the sheer size of this deal worried him. The results could make or break his career. Knowing that he needed expert help, he reached out to me, his mentor. Since Rahul had the reputation of being a continuous learner who worked hard to implement advice, I readily agreed to help. We met at a newly opened coffee shop the next day. After listening to Rahul's summary of the situation, I said, "All negotiations are not the same."

Negotiating successfully involves these key factors:

- Deploying Competencies

- Understanding the Big Picture

- Extensive Preparation & Planning

- Flawless Execution

Here are a few concrete steps you can take on your path to successful negotiations:

1. Build and Deploy relevant competencies: Excellent negotiation skills and experience are crucial for success. Be aware of your strengths and weaknesses as a negotiator. Build on your strengths and tackle glaring weaknesses. Strengthen your team by adding people who can cover some of your weaknesses. For example, if you need domain knowledge in a relevant area, take along a subject matter expert. Invite one of your company's legal experts to help you with contract terms.

2. Understand the Big Picture: *Ask yourself and your team these questions:*

- *Is this a new customer to your company, or one where you've had a long-term business relationship?*

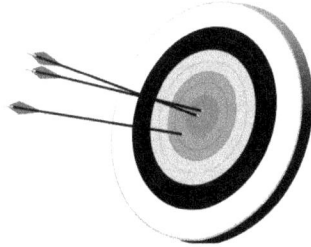

- *How important is this deal to your company? Does it have strategic value?*

3. Prepare Extensively: *A well-known negotiation truism states that the party that asks more questions is more successful in negotiations. Take the time to understand the customer's needs and how strong your competition is. Ask these questions:*

- *What are our highest priority goals in this negotiation?*

- *Putting ourselves in the customer's seat, what do we believe are the client's most important goals? Employing empathy, or asking a team member to play the role of devil's advocate is extremely useful.*

- *What will the customer gain by working with you? What can they lose?*

- *What are your strengths and weaknesses in the negotiation? What are those of the other party?*

- *What are the terms and conditions that could make either you or the other party walk away? If this negotiation were to fail, what would be your options? In negotiation terminology, this is referred to as BATNA (Best Alternative to Negotiated Agreement).*

3.1 Learn from past negotiations: *Ask yourself: How did your past negotiations go? What worked well? What mistakes did you make? Have you negotiated with the same client in the past? If so, what were your learnings? Note down these points to consider in this negotiation.*

3.2 Strive for win-win results: *Dr. Stephen Covey famously wrote on negotiation: "In the long run, if it is a win for only one of us, we both lose. Win-win is the only real alternative in most situations."*

Your aim should be to extract the best possible deal without damaging the relationship.

3.3 Actively look for creative ways of understanding client needs: *Negotiation need not always be a zero-sum game where concessions made by one party necessarily hurt the other.*

Barbara Porter, a good friend, beautifully explained this concept in terms of a freshly baked pie. Some people may go into negotiations trying to get all of it. Others try to get to an even 50/50 split. Knowing what is important to the party you are negotiating with is essential to creating a win/win situation, the ideal outcome of any negotiation.

Maybe one party loves the fruit filling, while the other loves the crust. Maybe one party wants all the whipped cream on top, and the other party doesn't want whipped cream at all. What if one party wants the pie plate more than the pie itself? These are all opportunities to define at and split up the "pie" differently.

Now, what if you're willing to give the other party the recipe used to make the pie? Look for opportunities to give things that don't 'cost' you much and maybe the other party will give you more parts of the pie that you care about!

How does this apply to project management? As vendors, we often negotiate with our clients on key factors such as Scope, Time, and, Cost. Client concessions in any one of these areas will almost always increase the probability of project success.

Let us assume that the client's priorities were in this order: Timely Delivery, Cost Effectiveness, and Scope of Work. If we, as vendors, negotiate hard on prolonging the project schedule, we are unlikely to make any headway. However, if we negotiate on the customer's lowest priorities in terms of scope, we are far more likely to succeed.

3.4 Find Creative Ways of Adding Value: *Building a long-term relationship requires the vendor to also make sure that the project delivers on the benefits expected by the client. On some occasions, it is a great idea to surprise clients with offerings or contract terms that they did not ask for. These may be items that will cost you very little but can add significant value to the client.*

* * *

Rahul took detailed notes all along. He asked quite a few perceptive questions along the way. As our discussion ended, his body language clearly showed that he was far more confident!

"I'm extremely grateful for your valuable inputs, Karthik. I assure you that I will use these practical tips, and update you once the negotiations are done," he told me.

Putting his learnings into action, Rahul carefully assembled his team. Knowing that he was not an expert in contractual terms, he included Mark Walters, a negotiating expert from his company's legal team. He also invited Zahara Khan, the team's CRM subject matter expert to accompany him to the negotiation meetings.

Rahul consulted with project managers who had achieved success with similar projects for other clients. He got valuable details from them on their lessons learned.

All members of the technical team brainstormed various inexpensive ways of adding value to the solution.

4. Flawless Execution

On the sunny day of the negotiation meeting, Rahul was a little surprised to see that WeBuildWell had brought along two very experienced negotiators. These negotiators had extracted large concessions from WinningEdge in the past. However, he felt confident since he and his team had carried out much more extensive research and planning for this meeting. Negotiations commenced with discussions on the project's budget. WeBuildWell's representatives insisted on the project being completed within a budget of $5.6 million. Rahul countered with a budget of $7.2 million. His boss had told him that the minimum figure he could accept would be $6.3 million.

Back and forth the parties went, explaining their points of view. It was exhausting. Rahul consciously stayed focused. He had read in a negotiation book that stamina and patience were key qualities to achieve a successful negotiation. A few hours later, WeBuildWell's representatives finally offered $6.7 million. WinningEdge's Procurement expert Mark Walters bluntly said the offer was much below par. He had noticed WeBuildWell's lead representative pulling at his collar, fidgeting and displaying signs of desperation. Mark was certain that he could push for a much higher price.

Rahul had two choices. One, play hardball, ignoring the negative consequences that such an approach could have on the long-term business relationship. Alternatively, he could convince his team members to adopt a strategy where both parties could win. He mentally chose the latter option. Requesting a brief break, he met with his four colleagues in another room. "Team: WeBuildWell has been a valued customer for over five years. I know that many competitors have been trying very hard to steal this account. Driving a very hard bargain may well push them into the hands of a competitor. Let's compromise. That way, we can win this deal and protect the relationship. Management will be happy with $6.3 million. At $6.7 million, we are getting 400K more than what we would have originally settled for."

While three of the team members agreed, Mark was still not entirely convinced.

He countered, "WeBuildWell doesn't know that we will settle for 6.3. Why don't we communicate that our management will accept nothing less than 6.9?"

Rahul was clear that he would not lie to the client about the number his management would accept. He knew that such an approach, beyond being unethical, would also damage his reputation in the eyes of his team members, and potentially his customer too. Mark's expression still made it clear that he wanted to push for more.

Notes from the detailed brainstorming exercises of WinningEdge's technical team came to the rescue. Rahul told Mark that the team would ask for dropping of requirement number 18.5.3 that would cost $65,000 to build. In return, the team would offer to include a "Chatbot" feature which would significantly improve the effectiveness of the solution. Since the feature was part of the company's reusable code repository, it would cost WinningEdge less than $10,000 to include the feature.

With Mark finally convinced, Rahul was happy he had achieved consensus. Back at the meeting, Rahul told WeBuildWell's representatives that he had the go-ahead to accept $6.7 million if requirement # 18.5.3 was dropped from project scope. Based on his homework, he knew that this requirement was not high on the customer's priority list. In return, he offered to include the "Chatbot" feature and explained how it would make the overall solution much more effective. He said, "At WinningEdge, you've seen how we aim to consistently add value to the solutions we deliver. This feature will help you connect with customers far more effectively. It is much more valuable to you than the requirement we are requesting to remove."

It was clear that WeBuildWell's representatives were very happy with this offer. With an agreement reached, the contract was soon signed.

Rahul's boss was extremely pleased with the results. The whole team celebrated that evening at La Mesa, a fancy Mexican restaurant.

* * *

What did we learn from this story? Systematically honing our negotiation skills and competencies, working on our weaknesses, extensive research, being creative with value-adding solutions, and flawless execution will indeed bring success. The magic will not happen overnight. It will most certainly not be easy. However, the investment will undoubtedly bring you rich returns. This approach worked for me. It worked for Rahul. And it will certainly work for you too! I wish you much success in enjoying the journey and the destination!

Recommended Reading

Negotiating Skills & Experience
"Negotiation Genius: How to Overcome Obstacles and Achieve Brilliant Results," Deepak Malhotra, Max H. Bazerman

"3D Negotiation: Powerful Tools to Change the Game in Your Most Important Deals," David A. Lax, James K.Sebenius

"Negotiating the Non-negotiable: How to Resolve your Most Emotionally Charged Conflicts," Daniel Shapiro

"Never Split the Difference: Negotiating as if your life depended on it," Chris Voss, Tahl Raz

Communication
"Charting Your Course for Effective Communication," Aileen Ellis, Peggy Wallis, Susan Washburn

Decisiveness
"Decisive: How to make better decisions," Chip, Dan Heath

Creative Thinking & Flexibility
"How to Have Creative Ideas: 62 Exercises to Develop the mind," Edward de Bono

"Negotiation Boot Camp: How to Resolve Conflict, Satisfy Customers, and Make Better Deals," Ed Brodow

Persuasiveness
"Verbal Judo: The Gentle Art of Persuasion," George J. Thompson, Jerry B. Jenkins

"100 Effective Persuasion Technique: Improve your Negotiation Skills and Influence Others," Helen Glasgow

The Big Picture
"Start with Why," Simon Sinek

Body Language
"How to Analyze people - Ultimate Guide: Learn Psychology, Body Language, Perception, Types of Personalities & Universal Rules," Jason Gale

Ethical Negotiation
"Enlightened Negotiation: 8 Universal Laws to Connect, Create, and Prosper," Mehrad Nazari

Empathy
"How to Win Friends and Influence People," Dale Carnegie

ABOUT THE AUTHOR
KARTHIK K RAMAMURTHY, MCA, MBA, PMP

Karthik Ramamurthy is a seasoned professional with 30+ years of rich experience delivering project success in four continents. He is author of the global bestseller, "Say Yes to Project Success" with a 1,000+ copies sold in under six months, and an Amazon rating of 4.9/5.0. He is also a contributing author to two other Leadership books.

As Keynote Speaker, Panel Chairman, Panelist, and Debater, he has addressed audiences of up to 2,000 in several countries such as the United States, Canada, Germany, Italy, India, Sri Lanka, Bangladesh, and so on.

Karthik is founder of KeyResultz, a Project Management and Social Media consulting firm which helps global organizations leverage global best practices to achieve project success. His qualifications include two master's Degrees (MCA, MBA) and the internationally-respected certification, Project Management Professional (PMP). He is a graduate of the prestigious PMI Leadership Institute Master Class, a program on Global Leadership with 30 participants from 16 countries.

He is also visiting faculty and workshop trainer to numerous prestigious institutions such as the Indian Institute of Management, the RBI Staff Training College, the Madras Management Association, Anna Institute of Management, and several leading colleges.

He has often been featured on Evan Carmichael's prestigious list "Top 100 Leadership Experts to Follow on Twitter".

Karthik is a multi-faceted personality: Bestselling Author, Sports broadcaster, Quiz (Trivia) Master (300+ quizzes across

30+ years as founder of Quizzes Exceptionally Done - QED), and Cryptic Crossword Compiler, Poet.

A long-time volunteer leader with the Project Management Institute, he has served in various local and global positions including Chapter President, Member of the Chapter Awards Excellence Committee, and the Ethics Member Advisory Group.

Contact Information:

E-mail: karthik@keyresultz.com

http://bit.ly/KarthikPMO

Phone: 91-984-060-1505

Twitter: @KarthikPMO

9

GOT A PROBLEM?
FIND A SOLUTION

Priya Patra

**We cannot solve our problems, with the same thinking
we used when we created them
– Albert Einstein**

It was a gloomy rainy day in Mumbai. The situation was no less gloomy in our team meeting that day. Our customer had come back with a list of 36 defects post our weekend deployment to production. Sound familiar? If you are a project manager in a software development industry you might have faced this situation at least once someday.

What kind of defects are these?

Could we have captured these defects earlier?

How did these defects get leaked to production post QA verification?

How do we solve these issues?

How do we ensure this situation does not recur again?

These were some of the questions that came up while we traversed through the list of defects.

We had a problem to solve: The Problem "Too many defects" in production.

Project management is much more than task management, resource management and scheduling. Projects today are now transformed to include complex combinations of sensors, hardware, software, data storage, and multiple protocols of connectivity to name a few. Projects we manage no longer operate in isolation but are part of a large ecosystem. They include a number of stakeholder's team members, clients, vendors, and many more. During its entire lifecycle a number of problems are likely to crop up.

Hence it is evident that a project manager must be capable of solving problems creatively and also able to learn and adapt to be successful. Project managers need to devise solutions by blending creativity and problem-solving skills as per the project's requirement. With their out-of-the-box thinking and experience, project managers can craft and implement their plan for any project they are working on.

PROBLEM SOLVING

What is Problem Solving?

The process of working through details of a problem to reach a solution. Problem solving may include mathematical or systematic operations and can be a gauge of an individual's critical thinking skills.

Steps in Problem Solving:

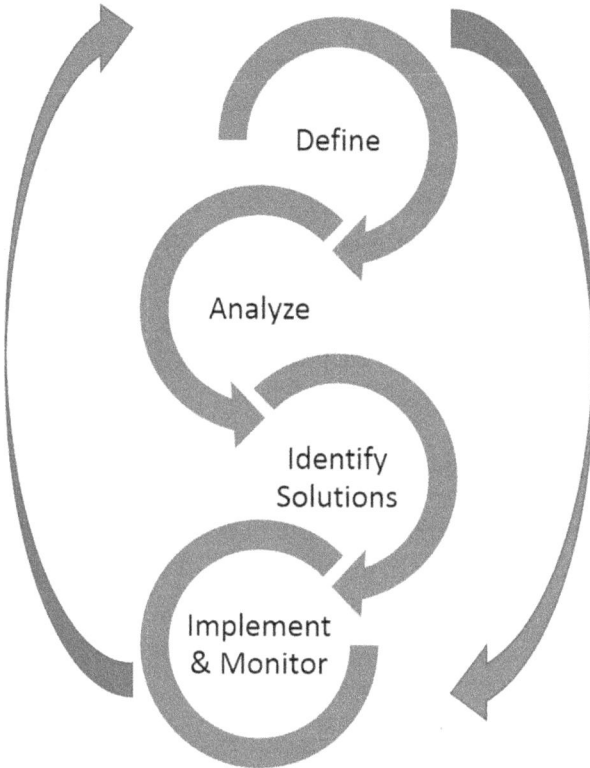

1. **Define:** A problem is defined to have a "goal" and an "impediment" which prevents one from accomplishing the goal. It is rightly said a well-defined problem is half solved.

   - Start with the current As Is situation

   - Explore the To be State or Situation

   - Ask yourself "WHY" and use an analysis technique to define a problem or to get to the source of the problem.

Write down the problem statement

Goal	Impediment

Defining a problem is often ignored or skipped to find a solution quickly.

In terms of goals and impediments, an attempt to define the problem helps with clarity, uncovering other problems and understanding the big picture. In agile terms it will help us to break the issue down into smaller manageable problems.

2. Analyze

- **Categorize:** Simple or Medium Complex category helps to identify if the problem is worth solving
  A complexity of a problem can be defined by the following dimensions

  - Details — number of variables and interfaces are unknown

  - Interrelationships — many interdependencies and interconnections exist

  - Effect — Affects multiple stakeholders

Dimension	Score (H-M-L)
Details	
Interrelationships	
Effect	
Complexity score	

If one of the dimensions are H the score is considered to be H

If one of the dimensions are M the score is considered to be M

- **Identify stakeholders:** Stakeholders are anyone who are directly and indirectly affected by the problem. Identifying the stakeholder's needs and expectations can help a leader understand the AS IS situation. Answering the following can help in identifying the stakeholders:

  - Identify groups/individuals who gain or lose as a result of solving the problem.

  - Why is it important for them to have the problem solved?

  - How would the solved problem affect them?

  - What do we need from the stakeholders?

  - What do they need form the solution?

  Once identified, analyze them. This can be done by categorizing them into the Influence/Interest Matrix as shown in the figure below:

  Some indicative questions which can help in categorizing are:

  - What is the power of the stakeholder?

  - How much influence do they have on the project?

  - What is the interest level of the stakeholder?

  - How much do they desire to be involved with the project?

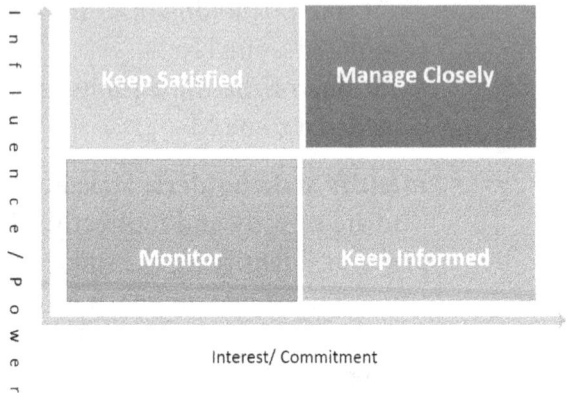

Chart: Influence/Interest Matrix

Once categorized we can develop a problem-solving strategy. The Power/Interest matrix can help in deriving a solution which would be accepted by the stakeholders.

3. Identifying possible solutions

Solutions to the problem can be classified as follows:

Confinement: These can be an immediate fix to prevent the problems from getting worse.

Corrective: Solutions which help in solving the problem at the grassroot level and prevent it from recurring.

Preventive: Solutions which prevent the problems from recurring.

One possible way to do so is as follows:

Question the question

Rephrase the question or the problem in hand for the solution. For example: the problem states there are defects in production that need to be resolved by tomorrow. Instead of asking how we can solve these defects within that timeframe and ponder the bandwidth, we should rephrase the question so it can further lead to other questions.

To solve the problem, the project manager could focus if the other project team members could chip in to resolve the defects. The team could also prioritize the critical defects for handy resolution.

Keeping implementation separate from listing solutions is what should be thought about in such scenarios.

- **Evaluate solutions:** We have the stakeholders listed out in step **Analyze**. This would guide us to select the appropriate solution to the problem. Solutions which satisfy the interest of all stakeholders is an ideal one. However, the one which satisfies the upper quadrant of the "Power/Interest" matrix would be a good enough solution.

Matrix for Solution selection:

Solution			
Stakeholder	Solution 1	Solution 2	Solution 3
Low Interest, Low Power			
High Interest, Low Power			
Low Interest, High Power			
High Interest, High Power			

Table: Power Interest Matrix

4. **Implement and Monitor:** Once we have evaluated the solutions and narrowed down on one solution, we brainstorm to select one or multiple solutions, we implement the solutions, monitor compliance, and follow through. We then conduct periodic checks to ensure the implementation is still compliant, and take necessary corrective actions to ensure compliance. These checks may uncover a new problem or residual problems. Repeat the cycle:

  • **Define — Analyze — Identify — Implement and Monitor**

3. A Problem isn't the problem, it is our attitude towards the problem

   Approach any problem in a different light. A 'Problem' is a problem because we look at it that way. How we approach a particular issue defines if this is a problem or an opportunity. Approaching the problem as an opportunity is an attitude which defines leadership.

   Leaders don't solve problems, instead they create opportunities. Instead of following the problem-solving approach, by continuing business as usual, it could be a catalyst to see how we can redefine the business. Instead of just reacting, we need to rethink and act.

   Few tips to change problems into opportunities.

   a. Start positively: Think you can. If we believe we can, we will achieve the result.

   b. Encourage creativity: Encourage your team to be a swiss knife thinker, think what new capabilities this issue gives you.

   c. Build culture to allow the team to fail: A safe environment is likely to bring in more creative solutions to the problems, thereby uncovering the opportunities.

d. Think long term: Focusing on an urgent problem does not help, a leader needs to focus on a long-term solution. Look for a long-term value other than the revenue.

e. Learn from the problems and the problem-solving process.

f. Make it a continuous process: Approach every problem as an opportunity. As we continue with this process this becomes a habit.

CREATIVE PROBLEM-SOLVING TECHNIQUES

- *Design Thinking Crowdsourcing*
- *Hackathons*
- *Lateral thinking*

Tips to transform to focus on solutions:

- Think in multiple dimensions and relationships
- See through ambiguity by defining the problem
- Use Systems thinking by focusing on long term solutions
- Leverage People, Process and Tools to resolve a problem
- Monitor, iterate and improve

If I had 60 minutes to solve a problem, I would spend 55 minutes to defining it and 5 minutes solving it
—Albert Einstein

ABOUT THE AUTHOR
PRIYA PATRA

Priya Patra is an Agile Evangelist and a Program Manager in technology industry serving the complete SDLC life cycle. Currently leading the Agile Community of Practice at organization level to percolate the Agile practices across the organization.

A mother of two, author, and blogger, Priya leads digital transformation programs. She is Employer brand for Capgemini, a global thought leader in Agile, Project Management and Digital.

She is an active volunteer for PMI® and has spoken in national and international conferences include PMI® Global Congress 2017, Chicago and PMI EMEA Congress 2018, Berlin.

Contact Information:

Social Media: Linked in Profile: https://www.linkedin.com/in/priyapatra/

Twitter handle: @priyapatra

10

MAXIMIZE YOUR TEAM EFFECTIVENESS

Donna Brighton

Team leaders are responsible for creating and supporting a thriving team — even in today's relentlessly changing environment. Let's review the four key insights to understanding team building below:

- Establish a successful team culture

- Perform a team tune-up

- Address demoralized or dysfunctional teams

- Utilize the 'not-so-secret' C's of team success

These four keys will help you understand how to build a powerful team that delivers great project results while enjoying the experience of working together.

CULTURE — HOW TO CREATE A
HIGH-PERFORMANCE TEAM FROM THE START

Culture is a result of a human being's craving for predictability and certainty. It develops when there is a consistent group of people (such as a team) and is shaped by shared history and the collective learning that comes from many experiences together over time. This creates patterns that define the acceptable ways to think and behave in response to various situations.

Cultures exist at multiple levels.

Macro-culture - the shared **culture** of a nation or state	The United States *Freedom*
Micro-cultures - a group of people living within a larger society who share values, beliefs, behaviors, status, or interests that are different from the macro-culture	Liberals Conservatives Disinterested *Many different points of view!*

The same is true within organizations. There is a macro culture that exists at the overall organizational level, and there are micro or sub-cultures within different departments, different locations or different teams. Any part of an organization that functions as a unique group can develop its own sub-culture.

All teams have cultures - the only question is whether it is unintentional, intentional, or hypocritical.

Intentional team culture: occurs when there is focused effort to define the team culture, then align and manage the culture, which is the team's values, beliefs and behavioral norms, in support of the project goals.

Hypocritical culture: is easy to observe in a team whose collective behavior contradicts the agreed upon values or norms. (Did you know that "integrity" was the stated #1 value of Enron? That is a clear example of hypocrisy!)

Unintentional culture: when there is no thought or focus put into creating culture, an unintentional culture emerges. It isn't good or bad, it's just not directed to create high performance or accomplish the project goals.

Establishing a new project team is a perfect opportunity to create an intentional culture. Since culture is a set of shared assumptions and beliefs that creates expectations for how to behave in various situations, take the time at the start of a project to define the culture rather than wait for it to happen on its own.

THREE STEPS TO INTENTIONAL TEAM CULTURE

1. *Prepare for Success*

- **Evaluate the Team** — understand the unique individuals who will be working together to accomplish the project outcomes. Use a personality assessment or spend time with the team, getting to know each member the old-fashioned way by asking great questions!

- **Define the Team Culture Required for Success** — what are the beliefs and behavioral norms that are needed to achieve success? For example, is it important to explore alternatives before acting, to pursue a standard of excellence and resolve conflict constructively? Is it important to have open and inclusive conversation, to be a good listener and communicate ideas effectively? How does the team need to behave to achieve the project goals? This is a challenging step because most leaders think more in terms of outcomes than behaviors. However, taking the time to define how to behave, and then consistently living out the behaviors and reinforcing them, is how intentional culture is created.

2. *Set the Stage* - create the conditions for success. There are three critical areas that require thought and clear definition:

- **What needs to be done** — define "what success looks like" and ensure that there is a shared understanding of the common purpose, goals, and approach to working. Whether the project is small or large, cast a vision to inspire the team.

- **Who is going to do it** — clearly define each team member's roles and responsibilities.

Rather than just assign tasks, build on strengths to maximize performance and engagement.

- **Guiding principles** — define the decision processes, issue resolution processes, team behavioral norms and communication expectations so that each team member is operationally aligned. This is where the elements of team culture are reviewed and incorporated into the team documentation.

One of the most important elements of successful teams is psychological safety. Project Aristotle was initiated to answer the question: "What makes a team effective at Google?" Research showed that how the team worked together was more important than who was on the team. The top behavior was safety which means that no one on the team feared embarrassment or punishment for admitting a mistake, asking a question, or offering a new idea. Make it safe in order to create a successful, high-performing team.

3. *Activate the Culture*

- **Get Acquainted** - Teach team members about different work styles and strengths. Use a personality styles tool to facilitate the conversation.

- **Get Prepared** - Coach team members in the agreed-upon behavioral norms such as safety, dependability, communication, and conflict resolution. What are the communication norms? How are disagreements dealt with in the team? Get clear at the beginning so you have a collective understanding of what is desired. This clarity ensures the team members understand the expected behaviors.

- **GO!** — the conversation about culture and behavioral norms is useless if it's not backed up with action. Reinforce the behaviors regularly in team meetings, feedback conversations and celebrations. Catch people doing things right and living out the culture. It's through the practice of team behaviors, mutual understanding, and shared learning that creates culture.

TEAM TUNE-UP

If you have a team that is already in place, it's not too late to get intentional about your team culture. Periodically assess your performance and use that as a basis for discussion and improvement. At any stage of your team's lifecycle you can evaluate and update the way that you work together.

Here are some areas/key questions to use to assess your team:

1. **PURPOSE** — Yes / No
   Everyone is clear on our collective purpose and the role he or she plays in achieving it.

2. **COMMUNICATION** — Yes / No
   We have a common language/understanding that enables us to communicate effectively.

3. **TRUST** — Yes / No
   We trust each other to follow through, to be fully present and share openly.

4. **SAFETY** —   Yes / No
   We can take risks on this team without
   feeling insecure or embarrassed.

5. **DECISIONS** —   Yes / No
   We make decisions efficiently and effectively, then capture and communicate
   them with anyone who is impacted.

6. **SCOPE** —   Yes / No
   We know what is in and what is out of
   our focused area of responsibility.

7. **CULTURE** —   Yes / No
   We have agreed on the way we talk,
   behave, and interact with each other.

NOTES:

_____

_____

_____

_____

_____

Once you've assessed your team, have a conversation about the actions you will take to make change. You can't create improvement without conversation and intentional action. Reach a collective decision about what will deliver the greatest benefit to the team, and make it happen.

There is a psychological principle that what you focus on flourishes or improves. Take time with your team to evaluate, agree on changes and then act. This "Team Tune-Up" will accelerate your performance and increase team member engagement.

The Not-so-secret C's of Team Success

- **Create Connection.** Teams are powered by people. People need connection or belonging. Create opportunities for connection to intentionally meet this human need through formal team building activities, shared lunch time (and space) or other social activities. Face to face interaction builds connection faster and more effectively. You can use IM to engage virtually: share questions and comments, communicate appreciation, share funnies and express yourself through the status line. Allocate a few minutes throughout the week to engage in caring conversations about what's going on with your team members. Social time is critical to team performance, but research shows lunch together is more impactful than team happy hours!

- **Connect with Purpose.** Being part of something greater than yourself is a key factor of human motivation. Not only do team members need to clearly understand the objectives and goals of the project, they benefit from understanding how what they are doing will achieve a greater purpose.

- **Communication.** Teams flourish (they are at their greatest level of productivity) when the members practice successful communication patterns. Researchers at MIT's Human Dynamics Laboratory found that **patterns of communication are the most important predictor of a team's success**. The best predictors of productivity were a team's energy and engagement outside formal meetings. Other patterns that predict success include:

  - **Talking and listening in equal amounts.** In a fast-paced environment, it may be challenging to make the time to hear from everyone. There are often team members who monopolize the conversation. This is an excellent example of a behavioral norm that can be defined when an intentional team culture is created.

  - **Team members have a connection with each other** (not just the team leader) In projects where the team is remote, it's easy to lapse into a "hub and spoke" communication pattern where the team members are communicating mostly with the team leader. Break that pattern and get the team engaged with each other.

- **Collaboration.** This is an intentional practice, that like culture, must be cultivated. It requires a team that shares, values, and then can integrate diverse ideas. Be specific how the team defines and practices collaboration, so everyone can succeed.

DEMORALIZED TEAMS

Teams become demoralized when their courage, confidence, or hope erodes. This can happen for many reasons including a significant loss, a failure, an overly optimistic goal or even exhaustion and burn out from an intense pace. Demoralized teams can no longer perform at their best and can negatively affect the morale of everyone around them. Here are some ways to overcome the impact and recover a demoralized team:

- **Be Real** — don't pretend everything is ok. Address the situation directly and encourage the team to process it. This is not the time to whine, grumble, complain or criticize! Focus on observable evidence and get a realistic understanding of the current condition. Perhaps emotion is clouding your assessment of the situation. Look at the facts and be real with the team.

- **Reconnect** — when a team gets frustrated and begins to lose hope, it's easy to degenerate into blaming each other. Rather than looking inward at the team members and identifying what's wrong with each one, connect with each other on a human level. What makes each person unique? What are their gifts and abilities? How can you see the positives in each other?

- **Renew Your Focus** — what is the mission, goal or higher purpose of the team? Sometimes problems overshadow the bigger goal. Spend time with the team reviewing what you are collectively accomplishing and why it matters. Help each team member see how he or she is making a difference with his or her work.

- **Celebrate** — find a win, something that did go well, and celebrate it. Remind the team of their greatness and the possibility of reclaiming it. It's human nature to focus on what's not going well. Sincerely celebrating a positive accomplishment, no matter how trivial, can recharge the drained energy of a demoralized team.

- **Learn** — step away from the issue and examine it objectively. What can you learn that can fuel future success? See the silver lining in an otherwise dark situation.

Proactively address a demoralized team before it spirals into dysfunction. Uplift the team members, reconnect them with each other and renew the focus on the goal to overcome the debilitating impacts of a demoralized team.

Dysfunctional Teams

Team dysfunction can manifest in missed deadlines, frustrated team members or the inability to make a decision. Dysfunction is any behavior pattern that undermines the stability of the team or reduces productivity and performance. It saps the joy from work and may begin a downward spiral for the team members. Fortunately, you can do something about dysfunction. Whether you are a team member or team leader, step up and be accountable for raising the issue of dysfunction.

How to address team dysfunction:

- **Focus on the evidence.** Don't assume that you know why there is dysfunction. Get to the root cause of the issue by determining the words or behaviors that are causing the issue. There are many symptomatic fixes that don't get to the heart of the problem. Stay objective and address what you are observing.

- **Take time to realign.** Realignment means getting in synch about what is true and what to do about it. Over time the team's composition, direction or focus can change. Perhaps your team got off to a strong start and just needs to be reminded of the goal, their roles and everyone's commitment to success.

- **Have a courageous conversation.** Beginning a conversation with assumptions ("Why are you trying to sabotage our team?") creates further dysfunction. Explain what you see, why it matters and ask the team members what they think. This gets them engaged in mutual diagnosis of the issue, so it can be solved. If a team member is not interested in solving the issue, then perhaps a courageous decision needs to be made about his or her future with the team.

Taking the time to proactively address dysfunction in your team will stop the energy drain and put you back on the path to success.

FINAL TEAM THOUGHTS

Set your team up for success from the beginning by defining an intentional culture. Then remain committed to that culture, say what you mean and then do what you say. When functioning well a team can synergistically accomplish more than the individual team members on their own. Teamwork allows common people to attain uncommon results.

ABOUT THE AUTHOR
DONNA BRIGHTON

Donna Brighton is an expert on building and facilitating high performing teams. She has been consulting for nearly twenty-five years and has done leadership, organizational culture and change projects in over seventeen industries. Donna holds an M.S. in Organizational Leadership.

She is a Past-President of the Global Association of Change Management Professionals (www.Acmpglobal.org) and served as a founders and member of the Board of Directors since its inception.

Donna was a volunteer leader within the Project Management Institute for over a decade. She served three terms on the Pittsburgh Chapter BOD, was on the First Standards Committee for Program and Portfolio Management, the Professional Awards MAG, the Nominating Committee, and served for four years on the Ethics Review Committee, including two terms as Chair. She is a graduate of the PMI Leadership Institute Class of 2003.

Combining a personal passion for wine and their leadership business, Donna and her husband Scott founded Leadership Uncorked. Together they facilitate leader forums and deliver extraordinary experiences for leaders and teams that combine leadership lessons with wine. From 200 people at the Ultimate Culture Conference to a ten-person executive team, they've delivered insightful leadership learning for wine lovers around the world. At Leadership Uncorked, Team Experience creates a lasting impact on boosting team performance.

Contact Information:
Donna Brighton

Founder, Leadership Uncorked
  www.leadershipuncorked.com

Chief Ideas Officer, Brighton Leadership Group
  www.brightonleadership.com

HOW TO USE THIS BOOK

This book has many uses as a self-leadership guide, training resource and coaching and mentoring resource tool. This book will offer these insights:

- Just in Time Information - As leaders we may be at different stages in our careers and need just in time information, reflection on how to move forward and tips on how to accelerate your leadership competencies and behaviors. Review my website www.naomicaietti.com for bonus material and downloads.

- Transformational Leadership Tips - This book is designed to have an introductory chapter to gain insight into leadership, leading and learning, how to transform and model your authentic leadership style, get unstuck and accelerate your career. Each supporting chapter will provide key leadership competencies with references to resources, tips, and more.

- Career Roadmap - Uncover the mystery of how to reflect, plan and act to establish your own personal career roadmap. Understand how a group of advisors like coaches, mentors and sponsors can be invaluable to leader's careers.

- Expert Advice - Eleven global experts have shared real stories, tips and advice in a standalone chapter focused on a key leadership competency. These experts are proven leaders with years of experience as coaches, directors, C-suite executives and consultants in the field of business, project management and leadership.

- Secrets to Success - Learn the secrets other leaders have discovered to thrive in their current jobs, jumpstart their careers down the right path and awaken their personal hopes and dreams.

- Leadership Competencies — Ten of the key competencies recommended for leaders by PMI, industry experts and aligned in the PMI Talent Triangle are shared here in standalone chapters. These ten competencies are Brainstorming, Coaching and mentoring, Conflict management, Emotional Intelligence, Influencing, *Interpersonal Skills, Listening, Negotiation, Problem solving, and Team building.

- Discover Your Purpose as a Leader - Learn how to deliver results through others; how to develop more leaders and add value to your organization.
  (*Interpersonal skills, as one of the ten leadership competencies is addressed and woven into many sections and chapters of the book.)

This book is a valuable resource and training guide whether you are new to project management, a credentialed project, program, portfolio, agile project manager, or an aspiring leader just kicking off your career. *Transform Your Project Leadership* will give you confidence to lead successful projects. You will learn about leadership, develop your leadership style and work toward practicing the art of leadership daily. Together let's begin your journey to take that first step to moving YOU towards your future leadership success!

ADDITIONAL RESOURCES

Please go my website www.naomicaietti.com/new-books, for additional materials that supplement and enhance this book. There you will find the following resources:

- Free personal growth and development guide to download to chart out your career plan and use to work with your mentor, coach and sponsor

- Links to the following:

    - assessment tools to assess your mindset/ behaviors

    - discover your leadership styles

    - useful leadership tips and podcasts

- Resources to use in journaling so you can jot down your thoughts as you contemplate the exercises in this book as well as reflect on your leadership journey over the coming months and years ahead.

ABOUT THE EXECUTIVE EDITOR

Naomi R. Caietti, PMP, CTM

Naomi Caietti is an award-winning business woman, widely respected global virtual thought leader in the project management community, a 2018 honoree in the new *Woman Kind* book by Ferguson & Fox about the 2017 #Celebrating Women Project, and has been given the 2016 Women of Influence Award from ProjectManagers.org, and 2013 Women in Project Management award from *pduOTD.org*. In 2014, Naomi founded her consulting company to meet virtual on demand business needs as a speaker, author and consultant. Naomi has been featured in national and international media/books including the Project Management Institute, *ProjectManagement.com, Workfront.com, Employee Engagement Network, ITMPI and ProjectManager.com.*

Learn more: For more information on purchasing a book, scheduling a book reading/ signing, virtual speaking events or finding more about the executive editor you can visit Naomi Caietti online at *www.naomicaietti.com* and *www.naomicaietti.com/new-books.*

Whether you are new to project management, a credentialed PM, or as aspiring leader just kicking off your career; *Transform Your Project Leadership* will give any professional confidence to lead successful company projects or initiatives.

www.ingramcontent.com/pod-product-compliance
Lightning Source LLC
Chambersburg PA
CBHW070725220326
41598CB00024BA/3301